Templates

Templates:
NOUN

Models **of**
NOUN   PREPOSITION

Style AND
NOUN   CONJUNCTON

Usage *for*
NOUN   PREPOSITION

Writers
NOUN

Stephen Lewis

broadview press

Library and Archives Canada Cataloguing in Publication

Lewis, Stephen, 1942-, author
    Templates : models of style and usage for writers / Stephen Lewis.

Includes index.
ISBN 978-1-55481-142-7 (pbk.)

    1. English language—Sentences. 2. English language—Syntax. 3. English language—Rhetoric.
4. English language—Style. 5. English language—Usage. 6. English language—Grammar. I. Title.

PE1441.L49 2014   808'.042   C2014-906593-0

Broadview Press is an independent, international publishing house, incorporated in 1985.

We welcome comments and suggestions regarding any aspect of our publications — please feel free to contact us at the addresses below or at broadview@broadviewpress.com.

North America
PO Box 1243, Peterborough, Ontario K9J 7H5, Canada
555 Riverwalk Parkway, Tonawanda, NY 14150, USA
Tel: (705) 743-8990; Fax: (705) 743-8353
email: customerservice@broadviewpress.com

UK, Europe, Central Asia, Middle East, Africa, India, and Southeast Asia
Eurospan Group, 3 Henrietta St., London WC2E 8LU, United Kingdom
Tel: 44 (0) 1767 604972; Fax: 44 (0) 1767 601640
email: eurospan@turpin-distribution.com

Australia and New Zealand
NewSouth Books
c/o TL Distribution
15-23 Helles Avenue, Moorebank, NSW 2170, Australia
Tel: (02) 8778 9999; Fax: (02) 8778 9944
email: orders@tldistribution.com.au

www.broadviewpress.com

Edited by Martin Boyne

Designed by Chris Rowat Design, Daiva Villa

Broadview Press acknowledges the financial support of the Government of Canada through the Canada Book Fund for our publishing activities.

PRINTED IN CANADA

For my daughters
Kerri, Tracy and Danie

Contents

Introduction

Rationale for This Approach

Readers and writers meet at the sentence. Readers process language on the page, or these days on a screen, moving from capital letter to period. Between those two visual markers—replicated in speech by rising and falling pitches—the language occurs in predictable syntactic patterns. And just as readers are aware of these patterns, writers compose their thoughts within them.

Good readers, intuitively aware of these patterns, anticipate the flow of language as they begin to read a sentence. They may not know how to identify a noun, but if they encounter one at the beginning of a sentence, they anticipate that a verb will follow, again even if they can't tell you what a verb should look like.

Skillful writers understand not only how to construct sentences that conform to the patterns of English syntax, including proper usage and punctuation, but also how they can enhance the effectiveness of what they have to say by playing to the readers' anticipation. They might delay the entrance of the subject, or they might offer what appears to be an awkward variation of usual word order.

Let's look at how those two techniques are utilized by a skilled writer in the last sentence, in bold, of the following paragraph:

I allow the spiders the run of the house. I figure that any predator that hopes to make a living on whatever smaller creatures might blunder into a four-inch square bit of space in the corner of the bathroom where the tub meets the floor, needs every bit of my support. They catch flies and even field crickets in those webs. Large spiders in barns have been known to trap, wrap, and suck hummingbirds, but there's no danger of that here. I tolerate the webs, only occasionally sweeping away the very dirtiest of them after the spider itself has scrambled to safety. I'm always leaving a bath towel draped over the tub so that the big, haired spiders, who are constantly getting trapped by the tub's smooth sides, can use its rough surface as an exit ramp. Inside the house the spiders have only given me one mild surprise. I washed some dishes and set them to dry over a plastic drainer. **Then I wanted a cup of coffee, so I picked from the drainer my mug, which was still warm from the hot rinse water, and across the rim of the mug, strand after strand, was a spider web.**—Annie Dillard, from *Pilgrim at Tinker Creek*

Notice two features of that last sentence. Begin with the syntax of "I picked from the drainer my mug." That should sound a little odd in your ear. More normal syntax would be "I picked my mug from the drainer." Why would a skilled writer like Dillard choose this more awkward-sounding word order? Two possibilities suggest themselves. One has to do with the word that comes next—*which*. That word is a relative pronoun. For it to have meaning it must refer to its **antecedent**,[1] a preceding noun or pronoun. We, as readers, look back and stop at the nearest candidate for this antecedent. If Dillard had chosen the more usual-sounding syntax, that antecedent would have been *drainer*. But that is not what she is talking about. She is talking about the mug, as the rest of the sentence will make clear. If we read *drainer* right before *which*, and then continue, we will be confused until we figure out we've identified the wrong antecedent. The second possible reason for Dillard's syntax is that it slows us down by calling attention to itself. That works in this case because Dillard is building tension toward the end of the sentence.

Building tension increases our focus as readers because we want to know where this syntactic train is heading. Look at how the rest of the sentence proceeds. First we get information about the mug, that it "was still warm from the hot rinse water." At this point, we do not know why we are being told this. Then we read "across the rim of the mug" and we still don't know where we are going, but perhaps we can begin to guess, given the whole paragraph that leads up to this sentence. One more phrase follows, "strand after strand." Then at last we get the verb *was*. A verb must be linked to a subject, and in English, the normal word order is subject followed by verb. Here that order is reversed. And the verb we encounter at this spot is the very colorless *was*, which doesn't tell us anything except that something existed. Finally, we arrive at the subject— "a spider web"—and we are rewarded for the trip through this artfully constructed sentence, which also has the virtue of underscoring the point of the paragraph, namely that Dillard takes the unusual position of considering spiders welcome house guests.

Templates encourages you to focus on sentence-level construction. It begins with simple syntactic forms and moves on to the more complicated ones, such as Dillard's. Along the way, it also deals with matters of preferred usage, a necessary adjunct to

---

1 Grammatical terms in **bold** can be found in the glossary.

the emphasis on style. Just as effective style enhances communication, less-than-acceptable usage detracts by creating unintentional awkwardness and confusion. In the Dillard sentence, we saw how a problem with pronoun reference that would have led to confusion was avoided, while at the same time a stylistic purpose was served.

That awareness of how the control of syntax and usage conventions combines to create effective sentences is what *Templates* offers you. English syntax is actually a good deal more complicated than it is the intent of this book to fully describe. Such extended analyses of the complexity of English syntax more properly belong in a book devoted fully and wholly to English grammar. That is not the purpose of *Templates*. Rather, this text aims at showing the basic structures of English syntax as an aid to improving your conscious control of sentence-level composition.

How to Use This Book

The structure of this book presents the syntax of English sentences in the form of templates, with necessary and optional function slots on the analogy of computer templates. It begins with the simplest two-word template and proceeds into increasingly complex structures. Each chapter describes the structure of the template, explores how it can be expanded with optional slots, provides guidance on stylistic options in manipulating the template, and analyzes usage issues. Exercises at the end of each chapter reflect these elements of each chapter.

The stylistic options and usage issues are, for the most part, the same no matter which template is being presented. For example, the stylistic concern of working with readers' anticipation, or the usage issue of subject/verb agreement, occurs in every template. Therefore, there is repetition of these topics throughout the text. The alternative would have been to offer separate chapters on the issues and to illustrate them within those chapters on the various templates. That approach, while avoiding the repetition, has the unappealing effect of divorcing the issues from the syntactic structures within which they are found. Further, the repetition serves to reinforce the guiding stylistic and usage concepts in each template, while the templates themselves provide contextual variation.

A Note on Terminology

This is not a grammar book. It does not attempt, as standard grammar books do, to describe the structure of English as an academic exercise, nor to prescribe acceptable usage in a rigid, judgmental way, as these books often do. Rather, this book intends to make students more aware of the syntactic possibilities that English grammar offers. In order to do that, however, we need to be speaking a common language, and that is the language of grammatical terminology. To that end, I offer here a brief overview of that terminology.

To begin with, let's examine the various ways in which that terminology attempts to provide a system of definition and classification into which the actual language can be placed. Perhaps you remember from grade school a definition such as "a noun is the name of a person, place, or thing." Grammarians call this kind of definition "notional," meaning that it looks to what the word means. As commonsensical as this kind of definition seems, it is often imprecise. For example, what do you want to call *fear*. Is it a noun? Well, it doesn't look like the name of a person or a place. Is it a thing? Maybe, but certainly not the same way that *table* is a thing. You can see, then, that notional definition can be imprecise. In its place, grammarians have suggested two other classification systems: function and form. Both of these are employed throughout this text.

The *template slots* I present are places in a sentence that must be filled with certain function words. As you will see in the next chapter, I divide these into necessary and optional slots. All English sentences include at least two necessary function slots: subject and verb. We can say, for example, that a noun is a word that can function as a subject; verbs function as verbs. Other functions include objects and modifiers.

Various grammatical forms can be placed in these slots. When we define by form we do not look at how the word functions. Rather, we look at the configuration of the word itself, how it changes in certain circumstances, or how it looks in terms of elements that are added to it, such as suffixes and prefixes. Using this method, we can say that a noun is a word that changes its form to indicate the plural number, usually by adding an -*s* at the end of the word, and that it often has certain suffixes, such as -*ment*, or -*tion*.

Similarly, we can say that a formal definition of verbs shows that words that add an -*s* in the third person singular are verbs. All verbs do this: I walk, you walk, he/she/it walk*s*, we walk, you walk, they walk. We can also, as with nouns, see that verbs often have a suffix, such as -*ed*. Comparing noun and verb suffixes, we have, as an example, entertain*ment* for the noun, and entertain*ed* for the verb.

This note is not intended to offer anything more than a brief sample of how I am going to use terminology throughout this text. Other grammatical features will be described where they occur in context of the larger issues in the book.

CHAPTER ONE

What Is a Template?

A template is the outline of a form—a form without the details. A template is like those pictures in children's coloring books in which the lines of a figure provide spaces to be filled with colors of the child's choosing, where the idea is to stay within the lines and to pick hues that make sense in the picture. For example, a person's hair is usually colored in black or brown or yellow, while a tree will have green leaves and something like a brown trunk. Of course, the child can choose to give the person in the coloring book purple hair or the tree pink leaves, and anyone looking at the picture so drawn would see the unexpected colors and decide whether the child artist's choice was interesting and provocative or simply inane or even disturbing.

Templates vary in how much flexibility they offer in accepting specific details. For instance, paint-by-number sets are similar to coloring books in that they provide an outline to fill in with color, but the outline is divided into numbered segments, with each number corresponding to a specific color. The idea is to dip your brush into the color of paint whose number matches the spot you intend to fill in, and then to paint that place, keeping within the lines as best you can. If you are successful, the painting you produce will look very much like the one on the cover of the box. In other words, this kind of template places a premium on replicating but discourages originality. In that respect, the child's coloring book invites greater creativity, although the results might be artistically less interesting.

You encounter templates in many different contexts. For example, word-processing programs usually include a wide variety of templates that can generate different written products, such as business letters, memos, work orders, envelopes, and so forth. If you have worked with these kinds of template, you know how fussy they can be in demanding that you stay within their "lines." If your content does not fit the slot into which you attempt to place it, bad things happen. Similarly, when purchasing items online, you often have to fill out a form, which is a template, providing specific details, such as your name, address, telephone number, credit card information, and so forth. Some of these templates can be very unforgiving. If you fail to fill in one of the slots correctly, the more unkind versions of these templates might just decide to return you to a blank form after you hit the submit button. A more user-friendly template will highlight the places where you failed to please it and give you another opportunity to satisfy it. But even this kinder template insists that certain slots be filled in with the proper forms. You do not have the freedom to decide to withhold certain information, or even to control the format in which you enter it.

Templates are found even where you would expect to find the most creativity. For example, popular music songs are almost always composed within one of three templates: the *AAA* song, the verse-chorus song, and the *AABA* song. The AAA song is a series of verses set to the same music but filling in different language for each of the units, indicated by *A*. A famous example would be Bob Dylan's "Blowin' in the Wind," in which each *A* verse begins with a question, which is answered in the refrain "The answer my friend..." that concludes the verse. The verse-chorus song alternates musically similar *A* verses with a contrasting *B* chorus, producing an *ABAB* structure. An example would be "The Battle Hymn of the Republic," with its stirring "Glory, glory, Hallelujah..." chorus. Finally, "Somewhere Over the Rainbow" is considered by some the most sublime example of the *AABA* song, in which two *A* verses precede a contrasting *B* section, which is then followed by another *A*.

These song templates have been employed by thousands of songwriters working in every style of popular music. The templates provide a predictable structure that the listener soon recognizes and waits for. This is true in terms of both musical composition and the lyrics that are made to match the music. Even though you might think of songwriters as creative free spirits, they still work within templates. If they didn't, their music would literally disintegrate into unrelated sounds. For example, one of the most rigid templates is the one that governs rap music. Its heavy rhymes and rhythms present a challenge to find language strong enough to stand out from the structure. These rules of composition apply not just to popular music, but also to larger works such as symphonies. The only difference is scale: the structure of a symphony is far more detailed and complicated than that of a simple song.

Verbal artists such as poets also work within templates. Some of these are centuries old, such as the sonnet form perfected by Shakespeare, with its pattern of three quatrains followed by a couplet. Even free-verse poets, who do not acknowledge the old forms, generally create a structure for their poems, which becomes a new template. Painters, too, paint within certain principles, which are visual templates, and dancers dance within templates of movements.

What does all this have to do with writing, and with the daunting subject of syntax? Simply this: English sentence structure can be—should be—seen as consisting of a limited number of templates that still permit a tremendous amount of flexibility. Let us now look at how the same principles of template structure outlined above apply to sentence structure.

English Syntax as Templates

The syntactic patterns of English sentences are templates. The templates are, in effect, a series of function slots that occur in a certain order within those templates. What distinguishes one template from another is the number, type, and arrangement of those function slots. As we speak or compose in writing, our minds fill in those slots in such a way as to produce sentences that our listeners or readers recognize as English.

To fill in these function slots, we have to know what words can be placed in each slot. When we listen to children learning to speak, we hear them fumble to find the right possibilities. As the children grow and hear more and more English spoken, they begin to internalize both the syntactic patterns, or templates, and the kinds of words that can be placed within the blanks in these templates. Perhaps a child will say, "Want up." The knowing parent will understand that the child wants to be picked up. Later, the child might understand the syntactic need for a subject function blank and produce, "I want up," or perhaps, "Me want up," having not yet mastered the distinction between the subjective form (*I*) and the objective form (*me*) of the pronoun. And so the child's language development begins. We can observe that even at this early stage, it is unlikely that the child will arrange those three words in a pattern that does not sound like English, for example saying something like, "Up want I," or "I up want."

Each of these slots performs a particular job within a template. For example, all of the templates we shall discuss include a subject slot and a verb slot. Other templates include, in addition, a subjective complement slot, or an object slot. Finally, all templates can be expanded to include optional modifier slots. These modifiers do not change the basic structure of the template but do change the meaning of a particular slot.

We need a name for the words that are placed within the blanks, and for our purposes we will agree with those grammarians who call them **constituents**. Constituents, as we are using the term, are words, or a group of words, that English allows to be inserted into a slot in a template. The names of these constituents might well sound familiar: **nouns**, **pronouns**, **verbs**, **adjectives**, and **adverbs**. Sometimes these constituents occur as single words. At other times, they are grouped in a cohesive unit called a **phrase**. For example, nouns can occur by themselves, as in the following sentence:

<u>Students</u> study <u>novels</u>.

Or we can add words to both of these nouns to form **noun phrases**:

<u>Many students</u> study <u>great novels</u>.

Similarly, we can turn the single-word verb *study* into a **verb phrase**:

Many students <u>have studied</u> great novels.

In addition, a **preposition** is a constituent that demands company—it must be followed by another constituent—its object. Together, they form a **prepositional phrase**:

Many students <u>in this college</u> have studied great novels.

In that sentence, the preposition is *in*, and it introduces the phrase *in this college*.

Table 1.1 shows which constituents can be placed in which slots within a template. The clause version of some of these constituents are not included here but will be dealt with in later chapters.

TABLE 1.1   CONSTITUENT OPTIONS IN TEMPLATES

Subject	Verb	Complement	Object	Modifiers
Nouns	Verbs	Nouns	Nouns	Adjectives
Pronouns		Pronouns	Pronouns	Adverbs
Infinitives		Adjectives	Infinitives	Prepositional Phrases
Gerunds		Infinitives	Gerunds	
		Gerunds		

As will be explained in the chapters that follow, the first four types of template slot—subjects, verbs, complements, objects—are necessary slots, meaning they are required to form part of the template in which they occur. In fact, all templates will have a subject and a verb; other templates will include a complement or an object.

As the name suggests, optional slots can, and regularly do, occur in all the templates, but they are not necessary parts of the templates in which they occur. However, they are "necessary" in a different way, as they expand the information that the template can communicate, while the grammatically necessary slots provide the structure in which to package that information.

One useful way to use this table is to think of each column as a drop-down menu in a computer template, for we choose from among these possibilities as we construct sentences, just as we choose from the items in a drop down menu as we work our way through a computer program. As we form the sentence, we choose a template. This is a complicated, yet at the same time speedy, mental process. Here the analogy with a computer template breaks down a little, however, because it seems that we are choosing the template at the same time as we begin filling in the appropriate words in the slots. Working on a computer, we pick, or have picked for us, a template within which we must work, and then fill in the blanks. Still, the principles in each case are similar.

But in another way, the analogy with computer templates is instructive. If we enter the wrong form in a computer template, let's say writing a date as 5/15/13 where the template demands 5/15/2013, our attempt will be rejected. Similarly, if we enter the wrong constituent in our sentence template, the result will be rejected in the sense that it simply will not sound like English. If, for example, we put an adverb in the subject slot, we will produce something that doesn't sound like English:

Quickly is useful in sports.

Here the adverb *quickly* is being asked to do a job it is not equipped to do. This template demands that its subject slot be filled with an appropriate form. We can fix the problem easily enough by changing from the adverb to the noun form:

Quickness is useful in sports.

Finally, the difference between computer templates and grammatical templates is flexibility: while computer templates accept only certain possibilities and reject others, with nothing in between, grammatical templates tolerate a range of choices, from those that are clearly preferred to those that are not acceptable, and in the middle of those extremes are some options that do not sound fully right or fully wrong.

Exercises

I. Templates

A. Listen to and study your favorite songs. See if you can identify the musical templates in which they are written. Do you hear an *AAA*, *ABAB*, or *AABA* pattern? Some other pattern? Try putting your own words to the music.

B. Browse through a book of poetry and see if you discover poetic templates. They are most easily observed in rhyme schemes, typically the repetition of the same sound at the end of a line. Or learn a little bit about poetic meter, and see if you can recognize this structuring device in the poetic templates. English metrical poetry is based on several different combinations of stressed and unstressed syllables that create distinctive rhythms. Try writing a poem, or at least a few lines, according to the template you have identified. For example, here is the outline of a Shakespearean sonnet template in iambic meter, a pattern of an unstressed syllable (-) followed by a stressed syllable (!). The rhymes are shown by labeling the same sounds at the end of lines with the same letter:

- !	- !	- !	- !	- !	A
- !	- !	- !	- !	- !	B
- !	- !	- !	- !	- !	A
- !	- !	- !	- !	- !	B
- !	- !	- !	- !	- !	C
- !	- !	- !	- !	- !	D
- !	- !	- !	- !	- !	C
- !	- !	- !	- !	- !	D
- !	- !	- !	- !	- !	E
- !	- !	- !	- !	- !	F
- !	- !	- !	- !	- !	E
- !	- !	- !	- !	- !	F
- !	- !	- !	- !	- !	G
- !	- !	- !	- !	- !	G

Compare this template with the actual Shakespearean sonnet below by reading it out loud as you look at the template:

> Shall I compare thee to a summer's day?
> Thou art more lovely and more temperate:
> Rough winds do shake the darling buds of May,
> And summer's lease hath all too short a day:

Sometime too hot the eye of heaven shines
And often is his gold complexion dimmed;
And every fair from fair sometimes declines,
By chance or nature's changing course untrimmed;
But thy eternal summer shall not fade,
Nor lose possession of that fair thou ow'st;
Nor shall death brag thou wander'st in his shade,
When in eternal lines to time thou grow'st;
So long as men can breathe, or eyes can see,
So long lives this, and this gives life to thee.

How exactly do Shakespeare's words fit the template?

C. Explore computer templates, whether in word-processing programs, spreadsheets, or online order forms. How rigid are they in demanding that certain kinds of content be inserted in particular slots? Are some templates more fussy than others?

CHAPTER TWO

The Intransitive Template

Subjects and Verbs

The two most important slots in English sentences are the ones grammarians call the **subject** and the **verb**. Together, and in combination, subjects and verbs create **clauses**. An English sentence consists of at least one clause, although it can—and often does—contain a number of clauses.

The term *subject* seems to appeal to your common sense, and you want to say that the subject of a sentence is what the sentence is about. As reasonable as that sounds, however, it is preferable for our purposes to think of the subject as a slot in a template that must be filled with certain words. We also traditionally say that the verb expresses what the subject does, or is, and once again, although this idea makes a certain amount of sense, let's instead consider verbs as the second of the necessary slots in an English sentence template.

Finally, and most importantly, these two items are linked to each other. In fact, you cannot say something is a subject, unless it is the subject of a particular verb; nor can you say that something is a verb, unless it is governed by a particular subject. Think of the relationship of these two terms in a way similar to combinations such as parent/child or husband/wife. In each of these cases, to say someone is the first term demands the second: a child must have a parent, a husband a wife, and so forth.

Thus a subject has, or is tied to, a verb, and a verb has, or is tied to, a subject. This kind of reasoning explains why in the **imperative** mood, which expresses a command, we understand that there is an unexpressed, but assumed, subject, as in "Wait for me." In that sentence, the assumed, unexpressed subject is *you*, so that if the subject were stated, the sentence would be "You wait for me." The fact that the sentence is not usually uttered that way does not alter the fact that we process its meaning by supplying that unexpressed subject.

The Basic Template

Let's look at how this combination of subject and verb creates a clause by examining the intransitive template. It is the most basic template since it contains only two necessary slots: a subject and a verb. Here is an intransitive template with the subject slot left blank:

_____walks.

Anything that can be put into that slot to produce something that sounds like an English sentence is considered a subject. Some common words won't work, however. Let's return to the example mentioned above (p. 19):

Quickly walks.

This sits uncomfortably in our ears because we are waiting for something else, namely the subject, to be introduced. *Quickly*, as an **adverb**, is not recognized as a possible subject. Now here are two possibilities that sound right:

The girl walks.
She walks.

The first sentence starts with a **noun** preceded by what is called an **article** or **noun determiner**, together forming a noun phrase[1] while the second begins with a one-word **pronoun**. Both comfortably fill the subject slot. You can add these subjects to the sentences above beginning with the adverb *quickly*:

Quickly walks the girl.
Quickly walks she.

Because the noun and pronoun were added after the verb, these sentences sound a little odd, the second considerably more than the first. Most English sentences begin with a subject, followed by a verb. That is the order we all anticipate when we start to read a new sentence. When the slots of the usual template are rearranged, the language calls attention to itself, creating emphasis. In this instance, the usual template order of subject followed by verb has been replaced by one that begins with an optional slot, filled by an adverb, then the verb, and finally the subject. Since you

---

1   Throughout the examples and exercises, "noun" is to be understood as indicating a one word noun or a noun phrase.

are accustomed to encountering the subject first, you have to work a little harder to process the language when you must wait until the end of the sentence. The more usual, but perhaps less interesting versions of these two sentences are the following:

The girl walks quickly.
She walks quickly.

The simple two-slot sentence above easily accommodates only nouns and pronouns as subjects. There are, however, some other possibilities for the subject slot, such as **infinitives** and **gerunds**. Both of these are called **verbals**, for the simple reason that they are derived from verbs. An infinitive is the base form of the verb, as it is found in a dictionary. In sentences, it is often preceded by *to*. A gerund adds an *-ing* suffix to the basic form. Both can be used as nouns, as in these examples:

Infinitive: <u>To win</u> satisfies.
Gerund: <u>Winning</u> satisfies.

Of course, in these very simple examples, the two-word sentence just barely fulfills our expectations of a fully developed English sentence. We will present more complicated and satisfying illustrations later.

For now, let's think of the subject slot as a drop-down menu from which we must choose to compose a sentence:

Subject   Verb

| Noun |
| Pronoun |
| Gerund |
| Infinitive |

| Verb |

To create a two slot intransitive sentence, you would pick one of the choices in the subject drop-down menu and a verb of your choice in the verb slot. Let's add a verb:

Subject   Verb

| Noun |
| Pronoun |
| Gerund |
| Infinitive |

| refreshes |

Now, let's pick some words that fit the required form for the subject slot, i.e., a noun, pronoun, gerund, or infinitive:

Noun	Exercise	refreshes.
Pronoun	It	refreshes.
Gerund	Exercising	refreshes.
Infinitive	To exercise	refreshes.

All of these sound like English sentences, though admittedly not very interesting ones. After all, how much semantic information can two words carry? We can add optional slots, as you will see later, to add content. But, for now, we are concentrating on this very basic subject-verb intransitive template structure.

Verbs occupy the second of the two essential slots in the sentence template. In contrast to the various forms that can appear in the subject slot, not surprisingly only verbs can fill the verb slot. Let's look at things that do not work in that position:

The guy <u>man</u>.
The guy <u>he</u>.
The guy <u>quickly</u>.
The guy <u>red</u>.
The guy <u>above</u>.

None of these sounds remotely like a simple two-slot English sentence. All but the first and the fourth could be the beginning of a more complicated sentence, and the fifth could be a response to a question in a specific context, but none of them works as a fully formed sentence containing a verb to accompany the subject *the guy*.

A simple test to see what form is capable of being a verb is to insert it into the verb slot of the two-slot template in two different ways. Using the first **person** pronoun *I* for a subject, insert the word as it appears in the dictionary. Then, switching to a third person singular pronoun subject, add an -*s* to the verb. This test produces obvious sentences using *walk*:

I <u>walk</u>.
She <u>walks</u>.

Trying this test with any of the possibilities above will produce nonsense, especially when the third person singular verb marker of an -*s* is added.

I <u>he</u>.
He <u>hes</u>.
I <u>quickly</u>.

He <u>quicklys</u> (or <u>quicklies?</u>).
I <u>red</u>.
He <u>reds</u>.
I <u>above</u>.
He <u>aboves</u>.

On the other hand, even a nonsense word can sound like an actual verb:

I <u>gezundicate</u>.
She also <u>gezundicates</u>.

I have no idea what one does when one *gezundicates*, but the word occurs where you expect to find a verb, it ends in *ate*, which is a common ending for verbs, and most importantly it adds the telltale *-s* when it follows a third person singular pronoun subject. These indications give it the look and feel of being a verb.

In fact, verbs exhibit a number of what grammarians call **inflections**. These are changes to a word's form to indicate grammatical facts, such as **tense** in verbs. This is not the place to go into inflections in details, but I can give a couple of illustrations. Verbs regularly inflect, or change their form, not only for tense, but for **voice** (active or passive) and **mood** (e.g., imperative or subjunctive) as well. You have already seen that all verbs add an *-s* in the third person singular present tense, as above. To change to the past tense, most verbs add the suffix *-ed*, although others change more dramatically, such as *think* becoming *thought*, which is another type of inflection.

One other absolutely consistent change is the addition of the suffix *-ing* to create what is called the **present participle** of all verbs, so that *walk* becomes *walking*. You probably note that the form of the present participle is exactly the same as that of the gerund. The reason for having two names for what appear to be exactly the same is that each does a different job; that is, each has a different grammatical function. As we saw above, gerunds are noun substitutes. Present participles, on the other hand, are used in the construction of **verb phrases**, as in the sentence "She is winning the game," and can also serve as modifiers, as in "She has a winning personality," where "winning" functions as an adjective.

What is important to note here, however, is that you know a verb is a verb primarily by its position in the template. It occupies a certain space, usually following the subject, where you expect to find a verb. But because verbs sometimes precede subjects, and sometimes are separated from them by optional slots, it is important to emphasize that we also recognize that the verb is partnered with the subject regardless of their relative positions. And verbs exhibit certain predictable inflections, confirming your suspicion that what you think is a verb is, in fact, just that.

Expanding the Intransitive Template

Clearly, we cannot say much with this template if we fill in only the necessary slots. One simple way to increase the information communicated by a template is to compound its constituents. Compounding occurs when a similar grammatical form is added in the same slot:

Jack went.

Now add another proper noun:

Jack <u>and Jill</u> went.

(Note: If you see where this example is heading, you are experiencing the kind of anticipatory reading that you as a writer should be aware of.)

Let's add an optional slot containing an adverbial prepositional phrase (i.e., a phrase containing a preposition and functioning as an adverb) that answers the question as to where Jack and Jill went:

Jack and Jill went <u>up the hill</u>.

We can add one more optional slot, another adverbial phrase, this time based on an infinitive and answering the question as to why Jack and Jill went up the hill:

Jack and Jill went up the hill <u>to fetch a pail of water</u>.

Because infinitives and gerunds are derived from verbs, they retain some of the characteristics of verbs. For example, as we will explore in more detail later (see Chapter 4), verbs take **direct objects**. In our sentence, the infinitive *to fetch* has *a pail* as its object, and the object itself is **modified** by the prepositional phrase *of water*. In any case, we now have added optional material to the two-word sentence with which we started, in order to create the beginning of that very familiar nursery rhyme.

A somewhat less common way to add to the subject slot is to include a special kind of phrase called a noun in **apposition**. This is a noun that occurs after (next to) another noun and provides additional, identifying information:

Jack, <u>an inveterate walker</u>, went up the hill.

Here the noun phrase in apposition, *an inveterate walker*, tells us more about the subject by providing more information.

Verbs can be compounded as well as subjects:

Jack walks.
Jack walks <u>and sings</u>.

However, building information into this template usually involves more than just compounding. Adding optional slots enables templates to say a lot more. These optional slots can precede the core subject/verb of the template, can follow it, or can occur between the subject and verb.

Let's start by looking at an adverb in an optional slot before the subject and verb:

<u>Quickly</u> the sun set.

Next we'll add a prepositional phrase after the verb:

Quickly the sun set <u>behind the hills</u>.

Now we'll insert two prepositional phrases between the subject and the verb:

Quickly the sun, <u>without regard for our feelings</u>,
set behind the hills.

Finally, we can add a simple time adverbial phrase at the beginning of the template:

<u>Last night</u>, quickly the sun, without regard for our feelings,
set behind the hills.

Notice, this is still an intransitive template with two necessary slots, to which we have added five optional slots: a single word adverb, an adverbial phrase, and three prepositional phrases.

Let's try one more:

I sleep.

Add the adverb before the verb:

<u>Peacefully</u> I sleep.

Now add the prepositional phrase after the verb:

Peacefully I sleep <u>in my bathtub</u>.

Insert a couple of prepositional phrases between subject and verb:

> Peacefully I, <u>in fear of nightmares</u>, sleep in my bathtub.

This time, let's add more prepositional phrases between subject and verb:

> Peacefully, I, in fear of nightmares <u>of dying from thirst,</u>
> sleep in my bathtub.

Finish this story with four more prepositional phrases:

> Peacefully, I, in fear of nightmares of dying from thirst, sleep in my
> bathtub <u>with the sound of water from the faucet in my ears.</u>

What should be becoming apparent is that prepositional phrases are frequently employed in optional slots to increase the amount of content a template can hold.

Another way to expand the amount of information an intransitive template can contain is to increase the complexity of the subject slot. Instead of inserting just a noun, we can substitute a verbal. So let's give this gerund an object and put it in the subject slot:

Subject	Verb
Winning the championship	satisfies.

We still have the intransitive verb template with a gerund as noun in the subject slot. But we have given that gerund its own object, namely *the championship*. Another quality of verbs is that they can be modified by adverbs, so let's give this gerund an adverb modifier.

Subject	Verb
Unexpectedly winning the championship	satisfies.

The adverb *unexpectedly* modifies the gerund *winning*.

Perhaps you can begin to see the possibilities that a simple one-word verbal offers in adding meaning to a slot in a template:

> To win satisfies.
> To win championships satisfies.
> Unexpectedly to win championships satisfies.

One final point worth mentioning here is that adverbs, more than most other grammatical forms, can move around while still doing their job:

> Unexpectedly winning championships satisfies.
> Winning championships unexpectedly satisfies.

Moving adverbs like *unexpectedly* in the sentences above usually just changes emphasis, as long as what the adverb modifies remains the same. In these two sentences, *unexpectedly* modifies the gerund *winning*. In the first sentence, the adverb comes immediately before the gerund, while in the second it follows *championships*, the object of that gerund. In that position, it is now unclear whether the adverb modifies the gerund or the verb *satisfies*, which it now precedes. Does the sentence say that the winning is unexpected, or that the satisfaction of winning is unexpected? This is a moment of grammatical ambiguity, which usually is something we would like to avoid in the interest of clarity. To eliminate the ambiguity, we could move the adverb to a position after the verb so that it would clearly modify *satisfies*.

What is important to understand here is that grammatical functions require relationships. To say that a word is an adverb is to say that it modifies something; that is, it is grammatically related to another element. There will be more to say on this point throughout our discussions.

Matters of Style

The usual English template offers a slot for a subject first and then a verb. In the intransitive template, as you saw above, the verb immediately follows the subject:

Subject	Verb
The girl	walks.

You can take from this a general pattern for English grammatical templates: the word order is going to be a subject first, followed by a verb.

This simple fact creates an automatic anticipation in readers. As soon as you read a capital letter at the beginning of a sentence, you expect to encounter a subject first, then a verb. Insofar as the writer satisfies that expectation, you will be able to process the flow of language as well as your understanding of the actual content allows. Does this mean that when you write you should always employ this usual subject/verb word order? Of course not. There are many reasons why you might want to vary your patterns. We will look at two variations: the first, and mildest, simply involves delaying the subject's appearance by preceding it with other material in optional slots; the second, and more radical, reverses the expected order by beginning with the verb followed by the subject. It is often combined with the first.

Delaying the Subject

To delay the entrance of the subject into the template, you add an optional slot at the beginning of the sentence. Various grammatical elements can fill that optional slot, from a one-word adverb, to a prepositional phrase, to a **subordinate clause**:

> I exercise.
>
> **Adverb:** <u>Enthusiastically</u> I exercise.
> **Prepositional Phrase:** <u>In the morning</u>, I exercise.
> **Subordinate Clause:** <u>Because my doctor insists</u>, I exercise.

As you will see later, this simple strategy of delaying the entrance of the subject slot into the sentence template can be employed to generate very complex sentences, simply by stringing together the optional elements into a series (see pp. 126–27).

Reversing Subject and Verb

Some centuries ago, questions in English were formed in this way:

> **Statement:** He told a lie.
> **Question:** Told he a lie?

Although this question template is still encountered occasionally (and always with the verb *to be*, as in "Are you happy?"), it has been replaced by another variation that employs the *do* **auxiliary**:

> *Do* **Question Form:** <u>Did</u> he tell a lie?

The same *do* form can be employed to answer the question with emphasis:

> *Do* **Form for Emphasis:** He <u>did</u> tell a lie.

More commonly nowadays, the subject-verb reversal (or *inversion*) occurs in templates that begin with an optional prepositional phrase. First, let's look at an intransitive sentence that includes an optional prepositional phrase after the subject/verb:

Subject	Verb	Prepositional Phrase
A huge old maple	stands	across the street.

If you simply reverse the subject and verb in this sentence, the result will be marginal English at best:

> Stands a huge old maple across the street.

However, if you move the prepositional phrase *across the street* to the optional slot at the beginning of the sentence, you produce a sentence that sounds fine:

> Across the street stands a huge old maple.

Matters of Usage

Usage concerns what is "right" or "wrong" grammatically. Most contemporary grammarians, however, talk about "preferred" rather than "wrong," insisting that usage questions are best understood as degrees of formality. To such grammarians, the terms "right" and "wrong" have a moral tinge they find inappropriate; this leads to a contrast between a *prescriptive* and a *descriptive* approach to language. With this distinction in mind, we will examine fragments, subject/verb agreement, and adjective/adverb choices in intransitive templates.

Fragments

A fragment is so called by grammarians because it is seen as less than a whole sentence. It is, in fact, missing something important. Here the analogy with computer templates can be particularly instructive. If you've filled out these templates, especially those you complete to purchase an item online, you know that they often have slots marked with an asterisk to indicate that something must be plugged into that spot. If you fail to heed that instruction, you are sent back: you must fill in that slot to have your completed form accepted. These templates vary in their degree of fussiness: some not only insist that something be put in the places marked as required fields, but also demand that only certain content is acceptable, such as entering a specific user name and a password when logging on.

While not that rigidly demanding, grammatical templates for the written language do include similar required slots. These are, of course, the subject and verb slots. In the spoken language, you may sometimes omit one or even both of these elements, but in writing, especially at a fairly formal level as in work for college classes, readers expect as a minimum standard that every group of words punctuated as a sentence will have at least one subject governing one verb. Whatever other optional slots you might choose to add, your reader expects you to meet this standard. In fact, you as a reader have the same expectation. We all read sentence by sentence, and we all share our sense of what syntactic elements appear between a capital letter and a period. As a writer, you can choose to ignore this standard, but preferably only rarely and even then only for stylistic reasons. In the latter regard, an occasional fragment knowingly inserted for emphasis can be effective. The emphasis occurs precisely because the reader's expectation is frustrated.

At this point, we will talk only about fragments in one-clause intransitive sentences. We will deal with clause fragments in later chapters on dependent clauses.

Fragments in one-clause sentences generally fall into two categories: subjects without verbs, or material that belongs in either another required or optional template slot. Here is a subject without a verb:

> Tuesday. We moved into our new house.

You read this statement of a date as a subject because it occurs at the beginning of a sentence template where you would expect to find a subject, and because *Tuesday* is a noun, which is what ordinarily occupies the subject slot. As a reader, you would then anticipate a verb to follow, but instead you hit a period. The experience is like being a passenger in a car that brakes suddenly for no apparent reason. The difference between the written and spoken language is the issue here. Spoken out loud, this fragment followed by the sentence sounds pretty good. All it really needs to conform to the minimum written standard is to delete the period, and continue into the required subject slot:

> Tuesday, we moved into our new house.

The difference between these two is small and almost disappears when both are spoken out loud. But readers rely on the visual cues of capital letters and periods; therefore, what is unimportant when spoken can distract and confuse a reader.

Many fragments are actually broken templates in which an optional slot, usually a modifying phrase, is separated from its template and offered as a sentence:

> Sentence Template   Prepositional Phrase
> The plot of that bestseller dragged.   From my point of view.

The prepositional phrase *from my point of view* is an adverbial modifier, which should be added to the preceding sentence template in an optional slot:

> The plot of that bestseller dragged, from my point of view.

As we have seen, adverbial modifiers can be moved around, so this sentence could be more effectively written this way:

From my point of view, the plot of that bestseller dragged.

Here is another template with an amputated slot:

Sentence Template	Verbal Phrase
My dog begs for his supper.	Wagging his tail.

The verbal phrase *wagging his tail* functions as an adverb that can be moved to various optional slots:

> Wagging his tail, my dog begs for his supper.
> My dog, wagging his tail, begs for his supper.
> My dog begs, wagging his tail, for his supper.

Fragments in the written language should not be hard to identify or to fix. If you remember that the minimum standard of a written sentence template requires it to contain a subject and verb, these broken pieces should stand out. Recognizing that they are optional slots of a sentence template, one that usually either immediately precedes or follows another element in the template, makes correcting them a simple matter of plugging them into the optional slot in any position that sounds right.

Subject-Verb Agreement

Agreement means that two related **constituents** are the same in their grammatical character. Subjects and verbs are constituents that should agree with each other in terms of their **person** and **number**. Because subject/verb combinations are the essential components of sentence templates, their agreement usually does not pose a problem. But there are situations where agreement is not easily determined.

First, let us understand that agreement can be based on either **notional** or **formal** characteristics. The notional approach involves meaning. If the subject indicates one thing, we say it is singular, and its verb should be singular. If, on the other hand, the subject involves more than one thing, we say it is plural and its verb should also be plural. The formal approach is based on whether the subject looks like a singular or plural in the sense that English nouns usually show the plural by adding an *s*.

Sometimes, however, these two ways of determining agreement conflict with each other. For example, here is a subject whose meaning is clearly plural, and yet it is treated as a singular. (Subjects and verbs are underlined.)

<u>Everyone is</u> here.

It seems clear that *everyone* must mean more than one, and yet the verb is singular. You don't have to understand why this is the case (although you can think of *everyone* as a combination of *every* and *one*); the preferred usage just evolved that way. Try putting a plural verb in this slot, and you will hear how wrong it sounds:

<u>Everyone are</u> here.

On the other hand, occasionally a subject that certainly looks like a plural takes a singular verb:

<u>Bad news stays</u> in my head.

The noun subject *news* looks like a plural because of its *-s* ending, and in fact in Shakespeare's day it was thought of as a plural, so the bard might have written our sentence as "Bad news stay in my head." If you think of the news as a collection of individual events, just as a book has many pages, the singular makes sense.

A few other common nouns, such as *athletics, statistics,* and *economics,* also have the *-s* plural, like *news,* and generally (but not always) take singular verbs. In addition, a number of foreign-based plurals create confusion and disagreement. For example, *data* is the plural of *datum,* and some very formal writers still observe that fact by using a plural verb with *data*:

<u>The data are</u> on my laptop.

Less formal writers would use the singular *is* instead, and both are considered acceptable:

<u>The data is</u> on my laptop.

Other foreign plurals include *media* as the plural of *medium,* and *agenda* as the plural of *agendum.* Language does change over time, and *media* is now well established as a singular:

<u>The media is</u> often blamed for showing excessive violence.

Still, some people would use the plural *are* in that sentence. In the case of *agenda,* however, nobody would link it to a plural verb. Its singular status has become firmly established.

Optional Slots between Subject and Verb

The confusion here arises in identifying the subject:

<u>One</u> of the puppies <u>runs</u> away.

or

<u>One</u> of the puppies <u>run</u> away.

When the sentence is reduced to its basic template, without optional slots, the subject-verb combination becomes clear:

<u>One runs</u> away.

You might well object that this sentence does not tell us very much, and that we need the optional slots to know we are talking about puppies, so that in terms of communicating meaning, *puppies* is the subject of the sentence. That observation makes some sense. However, usage depends on grammatical relationships, not what the sentence is "about." When the prepositional phrase is added in an optional slot after the subject, the object of the preposition seems to be the subject of the verb that follows it, merely because of its position. In this case, we are drawn to consider *puppies*, the object of the preposition, as the subject of the verb. We identify possible subjects by looking for forms that usually fill that slot, and nouns and pronouns are the most common candidates. *Puppies*, with its plural –*s*, is obviously a noun, and it comes right before the verb. The temptation, then, is to consider it the subject and make the verb plural to agree with it. Doing so, however, is to confuse the apparent subject with the grammatical one. A way to think about this problem is to remember, as pointed out earlier, that every element in a template has a job to do, some required, some optional; no grammatical entity just hangs out, occupying space. Therefore, if you want to say that *puppies* is the subject of the verb, what job are you going to give *one*? On the other hand, if you properly identify *puppies* as the object of the preposition, you still have *one* to assign the job of subject of the verb.

Compound Subjects

Sometimes, as you saw earlier, the subject slot is occupied by two or more elements. If the elements are joined by *and*, they are construed as plural and govern a plural verb.

<u>You and I run</u> for the remaining seat on the student council.

However, if they are joined by *either* or *neither*, and if they differ in number or person, a problem arises:

Either <u>she</u> or <u>I</u> *(run, runs)* for the remaining seat on the student council.

Which is right? This is a case where logic doesn't help, and an arbitrary choice has to be made. Simply stated, one verb cannot agree with two grammatically different subjects (third and first person). The preferred choice is to have the verb agree with the subject closest to it because that choice just sounds a little better:

> Either she or <u>I run</u> for the remaining seat on the student council.
> or
> Either I or <u>she runs</u> for the remaining seat on the student council.

In truth, neither version sounds particularly good, and as a matter of style it might be wise to construct the sentence differently to avoid the problem.

Here and *There* in the Subject Slot

English sentences typically begin with a noun or pronoun in the subject slot of the template, followed by a verb. When that order is reversed, particularly when the adverbs *here* or *there* occupy the subject slot, you are tempted to treat the subject as singular, when in fact the true subject follows the verb. You often hear

> Here <u>is Tom, Dick, and Harry</u>.

when the preferred usage would be

> Here <u>are Tom, Dick, and Harry</u>.

In this case the adverb *here* occupies the slot in the intransitive verb slot immediately before the verb, where we expect to find the subject. Consequently, we tend to treat the adverb as a subject, and because it has no sign of being a plural we make the verb singular to agree with it. On the other hand, the preferred usage recognizes that the actual subject in this sentence follows the verb. If we put this sentence into the more normal subject-first word order, the preferred choice would be obvious:

> <u>Tom, Dick, and Harry are</u> here.

Phrased that way, few would choose the singular verb *is*:

> <u>Tom, Dick, and Harry is</u> here.

The same usage problem arises with the adverb *there* in the subject slot:

> <u>There is</u> Tom, Dick, and Harry.

And in both instances, the problem is compounded by the tendency to contract the verb and attach it to the adverb:

Here's (there's) Tom, Dick, and Harry.

Other areas of subject-verb agreement are discussed in the later chapters on subordinate clauses (Chapters 8–10), because the usage problems occur in more complicated, multi-clause templates.

Adjectives and Adverbs

Because the basic intransitive template provides so little information, it is often filled out with optional material, as we saw above. One of the simplest ways to expand the message carried by the template is to follow the verb with an optional modifier. That modifier, since it is grammatically linked to the verb, should be an adverb. A common usage mistake is to insert an adjective instead of the preferred adverb, as we see in the following:

My old car runs good.

Good is an adjective; the preferred usage would be an adverb:

My old car runs well.

[Note: *well*, in the sense of good health, can also be an adjective, as in "After her illness, she is now well."]

I did terrible on the test.

The adjective *terrible* should be replaced with its adverbial form:

I did terribly on the test.

We will see a similar confusion between adverbs and adjectives in the next chapter when we look at the linking verb template. In that case, the usage preference will turn out to be adjectives rather than adverbs.

Exercises

I. Subjects

Think of possible subjects as a list in a drop-down menu:

Noun
Pronoun
Gerund
Infinitive

Pick one possibility from the drop-down list to create sentences with the following words in the verb slot:

1.

Noun
Pronoun
Gerund
Infinitive

   sits.

2.

Noun
Pronoun
Gerund
Infinitive

   stands.

3.

Noun
Pronoun
Gerund
Infinitive

   succeeds.

4.

Noun
Pronoun
Gerund
Infinitive

   disappears.

5. Compose five sentences using these drop-down choices with your own verbs.

1. _____

2. _____

3. _____

4. _____

5. _____

II. Optional Slots

Fill in the optional slots with the specified forms.

Adverb   **Subject**   **Verb**

1. _____   the car   stopped.

2. **Prepositional Phrase**   **Subject**   **Verb**

   _____   I   walk.

3. **Subject**   **Verb**   **Prepositional Phrase**

   She   sings   _____.

4. **Subject**   **Verb**   **Adverb**   **Prepositional Phrase**

   She   sings   _____ _____.

5. **Prepositional Phrase**   **Prepositional Phrase**   **Subject**   **Verb**

   _____   _____   the plane   rose.

III. Subject/Verb Inversion

Fill in the blank slots with appropriate words or phrases of your choice.

1. **Adverb**   **Verb**   **Subject**

   Quickly   _____   the storm.

2. **Prepositional Phrase**   **Verb**   **Subject**

   On top of the hill   is   _____.

3. **Prepositional Phrase**   **Prepositional Phrase**   **Verb**   **Subject**

   Behind the door   in the dark   _____   the body.

4. **Adverb**   **Prepositional Phrase**   **Verb**   **Subject**

   _____   _____   came   Jack.

IV. Subject-Verb Agreement

Choose the verb that best agrees with the subject. Do any of these sound right both ways? If so, why?

1. One of the students (has, have) not registered for this course.
2. Several of the games (was, were) won in the last minute.
3. Everyone among the spectators (cheer, cheers) for the home team.
4. The data for the project (has, have) just arrived.
5. A new course in economics (appears, appear) in the spring schedule.
6. Either my brother or I (is, am) in line for the next promotion at the factory.
7. Jack and Mary, along with Mike, (is, are) at the party by now.
8. One of my problems (sicken, sickens) me.
9. Here (is, are) my friend with his dogs.
10. There (is, are) the rest of my crew.

V. Adjective/Adverb

Choose the preferred option in the following:

1. At the prom, we danced (wonderfully, wonderful) all night.
2. Jack walked (careful, carefully) over the ice.
3. In the afternoon, the rain came (suddenly, sudden).
4. Before you act, think (clearly, clear) about the consequences.
5. The dog's tail wagged (energetic, energetically).
6. The cat purred (gentle, gently) on my lap.
7. At the beach, the surf roared (furiously, furious).
8. Mary struggled (mighty, mightily) with the new computer program.

CHAPTER THREE

The Linking Template

The linking template has three required slots. Of course, it must have a subject slot and a verb slot. To these it adds what grammarians call the **subjective complement** slot.

Grammatical terms sometimes clearly explain the concept they express, and sometimes seem to bear little relationship to that concept. In the case of the linking verb template, the terms are of the former variety: they rather clearly relate to the grammatical concept they express. To *complement* (as opposed to *compliment*) is to complete or add to something. For example, if you said, "My new shoes complement my spring outfit," you would mean that the shoes add to or complete the look of the outfit. In much the same way, a subjective complement in the linking template communicates additional information about the subject to which it is linked. The term **linking verb** accurately describes what the word in that slot does. It links, or holds together, the subject and the subjective complement.

The Basic Template

Here is what a linking template looks like:

Subject   Linking Verb   Subjective Complement

Notice we have qualified the verb slot by saying that it must be a certain type of verb. In fact, there are a very limited number of verbs that can occupy that slot. We will examine that list later in the chapter. For now, let us concentrate on the structure of the template. Since the verb *be* is the most common linking verb, we will use it in our first examples.

The forms in the subjective complement slot occur in two varieties. One restates the subject by using another noun or a pronoun:

Noun Subject	Linking Verb	Noun Subjective Complement
My cousin Jill	is	a carpenter.

Note that if a pronoun is placed in the subjective complement slot, it creates a usage issue discussed later in this chapter (p. 53).

In the second variety for the linking verb template, an adjective occurs in the subjective complement to tell us something about the subject:

Noun Subject	Linking Verb	Adjective Subjective Complement
My cousin Jill	is	happy.

Notice that, in this variety, the form in the subjective complement must be an adjective rather than an adverb because it is linked to, and modifies, the noun subject. Adverbs do not modify nouns or pronouns; therefore, they cannot modify the subject of a linking verb template. When they occur in the subjective complement slot, the reader feels that the linking verb rather than the noun or pronoun subject is being modified. We will examine this issue more fully later in the chapter (pp. 50–53).

We can now visualize the three-slot linking-verb template with drop-down menus for subject and subjective complement:

Noun		Verb		Noun
Pronoun				Pronoun
Gerund				Adjective
Infinitive				

Expanding the Linking Verb Template

Having established the basic elements of the three-slot linking verb template, let's start expanding each of the slots with modifiers, starting with this simple sentence:

Subject	**Verb**	**Subjective Complement**
Jill	is	a carpenter.

First, add a noun phrase in apposition to the subject:

Subject	**Verb**	**Subjective Complement**
Jill, my favorite cousin,	is	a carpenter.

Now let's put a prepositional phrase after the subject:

Subject	Phrase	Verb	Complement
Jill, my favorite cousin	on my mother's side,	is	a carpenter.

Add two more optional slots, an adverb after the linking verb itself and a prepositional phrase after the subjective complement:

Subject	Phrase	Verb	Adverb
Jill, my favorite cousin	on my mother's side,	is	unexpectedly

Complement	Phrase
a carpenter	of wonderful ability.

You have seen in the previous chapter how optional slots added to the basic template produce sentences that can communicate a great deal of nuanced information. The essential building blocks, however, are the required template slots.

As you also saw in the previous chapter, gerunds and infinitives can function as nouns. Because they can occur in any subject slot in any template, we will find them as subjects in linking verb sentences:

Gerund Subject	Verb	Subjective Complement
Winning	is	enjoyable.
Infinitive Subject	Verb	Subjective Complement
To win	is	enjoyable.

We now know that these verbals retain characteristics of verbs, meaning, for example, they can have objects:

Gerund Subject	Object	Verb	Subjective Complement
Winning	the championship	is	enjoyable.
Infinitive Subject	Object	Verb	Subjective Complement
To win	the championship	is	enjoyable.

Additional modifiers, as usual, can be added to produce complicated sentences such as this one:

To convincingly win the championship after losing five games at the beginning of the season is enjoyable beyond our wildest expectations.

If we reduce this sentence to its simple three slot linking verb template, we have the following:

> To win is enjoyable.

Adding the object of the verbal produces this:

> To win the championship is enjoyable.

Now we insert the three prepositional phrases in the subject slot:

> To win the championship after losing five games at the beginning of the season is enjoyable.

Finally, we add the prepositional phrase after the adjective subjective complement:

> To win the championship after losing five games at the beginning of the season is enjoyable beyond our wildest expectations.

Other Linking Verbs

Thus far, we have been using forms of *be* as the linking verb in our examples because it is the most common verb in that slot. However, English does allow a small number of other verbs to occupy that position. The other candidates to fill the verb slot in the linking verb template include the following:

Linking verb	Subject	Verb	Subjective Complement
appear	That new movie	appears	interesting.
become	Seeds	become	flowers.
feel	I	feel	happy.
grow	The day	grows	cloudy.
look	She	looks	marvelous.
prove	The problem	proved	difficult.
remain	The captured prisoner	remained	an enemy.
seem	That	seems	an imposition.
smell	Those flowers	smell	sweet.
stay	We	stay	optimistic.
sound	That car engine	sounds	terrible.
taste	My new recipe	tastes	awful.
turn	The snow storm	turned	nasty.

In the next chapter, we will see how some of these verbs also appear in the transitive template.

One example will suffice to show how sentences with these verbs, like those we saw using *be*, can be developed by adding material in optional slots. Let's start by adding an adverbial prepositional phrase in front of the last model sentence:

PP	Subject	Verb	Complement
In the morning,	the snow storm	turned	nasty.

Now, a single word adverb before the verb:

PP	Subject	Adverb	Verb	Complement
In the morning,	the snow storm	rapidly	turned	nasty.

Next, a prepositional phrase after the adjective subjective complement:

PP	Subject	Adverb	Verb	Complement
In the morning,	the snow storm	rapidly	turned	nasty
PP				
beyond predictions.				

Finally, another prepositional phrase at the end of the sentence:

PP	Subject	Adverb	Verb	Complement
In the morning,	the snow storm	rapidly	turned	nasty
PP	PP			
beyond predictions	of the weatherman.			

What bears repetition, as you shall see throughout this book, is how English syntax permits the construction of complicated sentences by adding material to the basic templates in optional slots. You will also see how the templates themselves can be added to each other to build even more complicated sentence structures.

Matters of Style

We can use the same stylistic maneuvers in this template as we did in the intransitive template in the previous chapter. For example, we can delay the entrance of the subject into the sentence. This strategy, available in any template, always creates tension because readers await what their sense of English syntax teaches them to anticipate, namely, the subject of the sentence. And creating a tension that will later be resolved is one of the goals of prose style.

Look at the example in the previous section where we added a prepositional phrase to the beginning of the template. We started with the unadorned template:

> The snow storm turned nasty.

Then we added a prepositional phrase at the very beginning in an optional slot:

> <u>In the morning</u>, the snow storm turned nasty.

Think about how that little change alters the way readers would process the sentence. They first read the phrase, which gives them a time reference. Something happened, or was true, in the morning. Having read that much, readers now want to know what happened, or what was true, that morning. The rest of the sentence provides the answer.

As we have seen before, additional optional slots can be placed before the subject. The longer the reader must wait to read the subject, the more tension is created. Let's add a few more to this example:

> <u>Unexpectedly</u>, in the morning, <u>before first light</u>, <u>with the sound of the wind against our windows</u>, the snow storm turned nasty.

Not only do these additional slots create more delay, and thus greater tension, but they also provide additional information that intensifies the message being communicated.

Matters of Usage

The most common usage problems in the linking verb template are adjective/adverb confusion, and to a lesser degree subject/verb agreement.

Adjectives and Adverbs

Problems can occur here because the linking verb template calls for an adjective in the subjective complement. To place an adverb in that slot causes confusion, because the adverb is seen to be modifying the verb rather than the subject, which of course is a noun.

The most frequent adjective/adverb combination that causes a usage problem in the linking verb template is the *bad/badly* duo: *bad* is an adjective and is the preferred choice in the subjective complement of a linking verb template, while *badly* is an adverb and the one many people feel is the right choice.

Consider this pair of sentences:

>Jack felt bad about the situation.
>Jack felt badly about the situation.

Which sounds right to you? The first? The second? Both?

If you are not sure, or feel sure that both sound right, you are probably in the majority of contemporary users of English. However, the preferred usage choice is unequivocally the first:

>Jack felt bad about the situation.

This is because, in this sentence, *felt* is a linking verb followed by a subjective complement, which demands an adjective, and *bad* is that adjective.

There are at least three reasons why people have difficulty with sentences such as these. First, like so many English verbs, *feel* can appear in more than one template. We see it here in the linking verb template. But in the next chapter, we will see it in the transitive verb template as well. Here is an example, for a quick preview:

>Jack felt the cold floor beneath his feet.

It is possible, though not likely, that we could put the adverb *badly* into that sentence:

>Jack badly felt the cold floor beneath his feet.

That sounds odd, because it *is* odd. It means that Jack's sense of touch wasn't working well, because the adverb is modifying the verb. However, to make the grammatical point that *feel* in this sentence can be modified by an adverb, let's try a more reasonable possibility.

>Jack certainly felt the cold floor beneath his feet.

That one sounds fine, and it shows that an adverb such as *certainly* can modify the verb *feel*. Therefore, when a reader or listener sees or hears the verb *feel*, only the recognition of the whole template determines whether the modifier near it should be an adjective or an adverb.

Let's explore this issue a little more by looking at the adverb *certainly*, as opposed to the adjective *certain*, in the subjective complement slot of a linking verb template. Compare the following:

>Jack felt certainly about the situation.
>Jack felt certain about the situation.

In these examples, the preferred choice of an adjective in the subjective complement is clear.

A second reason for the confusion is that another common problem, as we saw in the last chapter, is using an adjective where formal usage prefers an adverb:

> Jack's old clunker runs bad.

According to formal usage that would have an adverb instead of an adjective:

> Jack's old clunker runs badly.

In the linking verb template, however, the preferred choice is just the opposite:

> Jack's old clunker sounds bad.

That usage is preferred to the adverb possibility:

> Jack's old clunker sounds badly.

A third and related reason for this persistent confusion is that the use of an adjective instead of an adverb in the intransitive verb template, as in the above example, occurs with great frequency, and we have drilled into our heads that adverbs, particularly those with the *-ly* suffix are "good" English, while adjectives without the *-ly* are "bad" English. There is a tendency to transfer such a sense from one usage issue where it belongs to another where it does not. Thus we think that words ending in *-ly* sound better in all instances, even when preferred usage says they are not the best choice. Grammarians call this tendency "hypercorrection": when users of a language try too hard to avoid one mistake, only to wind up making another.

Other linking verbs aside from *be* pose similar adjective/adverb problems. Compare the following pairs:

> That new recipe tasted terribly.
> That new recipe tasted terrible.

> Those flowers smell sweetly.
> Those flowers smell sweet.

In both cases the second sentence in the pair, the one with the adjective in the subjective complement slot, is preferred.

Here's another particularly troublesome pair:

> The runner appeared slow.
> The runner appeared slowly.

Can you see that both can be correct? In the first, we are dealing with a linking verb template, and the adjective *slow* is modifying the subject *runner*. In the second, we have an intransitive template, and the adverb *slowly* modifies the verb, suggesting that the runner was coming into sight at a slow pace.

A final complication in this example is that contemporary English often drops the *-ly* suffix from one syllable adverbs such as *slow*, so that to some it is acceptable to say, for example, "The runner ran slow."

The Case of Pronouns in the Subjective Complement

Not only does the choice between adjectives or adverbs cause a usage issue. In a similar vein, we have to decide the **case** of personal pronouns in subjective complements. Grammarians classify case according to the function of the word. Is it a subject? Then it is **nominative**, or subjective, case. Is it an object? Then it is **objective** case. Some grammarians include a third possibility, which they call the "possessive" case, which occurs when the word in question is functioning as an adjective indicating possession, as in "*my* book." Nouns theoretically also can be put into these case categories but since they do not change their form to reflect their case (aside from the addition of a possessive *-s*, as in *the girl's shoes*), we don't need to worry about them. Personal pronouns, however, do change form for different case situations, and thus can cause a problem.

This issue is routinely encountered when an individual knocks on a door, and the person on the other side of the door asks, "Who is it?" Many people in that situation would respond, not by giving their name but by saying, "It's me," assuming that the other person would recognize their voice. Similar situations occur on the phone, too.

The grammar issue, though, has nothing to do with the question of voice recognition. Rather, it involves the nature of a subjective complement. In our example, we are dealing with a linking verb template, with the pronoun *It* as the subject, the linking verb *is*, represented here by the contracted form *'s*, and the pronoun subjective complement *me*. All of this, no doubt, seems clear enough. But here's the issue: linking verbs do not take objects. A noun or pronoun in the subjective complement restates the subject. Consequently, the grammatical rule of agreement applies, meaning that the subject and the subjective complement should agree with, be in the same form as, each other. In this instance, both must be in the nominative case; yet *I* is in the nominative case while *me* is in the objective case in our example. To resolve the problem, we get this formally preferred answer to the simple question of who is knocking at the door:

It is I.

We know, however, that in real life, few people would say that. It sounds insufferably formal.

Subject-Verb Agreement

Whenever an optional slot occurs between the subject and the verb we are waiting for, there is a possibility of an agreement problem, especially if the optional material is a prepositional phrase. This is because prepositional phrases always end with a noun, or noun equivalent object, and therefore we are tempted to think that the prepositional phrase's object governs the verb rather than the actual grammatical subject:

> One of the possibilities (are, is) plausible.

In this example, it might not be too difficult to ignore the nearest noun—*possibilities*—and see that the verb connects to the subject *one*. And since *one* is clearly singular, the verb should be so as well:

> One of the possibilities is plausible.

Notice, however, what happens if we add another prepositional phrase with another plural noun object:

> One of the dozens of possibilities (are, is) plausible.

Now the pull toward *possibilities* as the nearest noun to the verb is stronger, while at the same time the more distant pronoun subject *one* does not as strongly demand recognition as the subject of the verb.

Add one more prepositional phrase and the weakening and strengthening tendencies increase:

> One of the dozens of possibilities in all the reports (are, is) plausible.

What must be remembered in all these instances is that in English syntax each grammatical unit can do only one job. Applying this rule to these sentences above, you see that the nouns at the end of each prepositional phrase already have their defined job: they are the objects of their prepositions. Therefore, they cannot also serve as subjects of the verb.

A similar rule states that every grammatical unit has to be doing something. It can't just be standing around with its hands in its pockets, gazing up at the sky while all of its colleagues are gainfully employed. In our sentences above, the pronoun *one* must have a job to do, and in these instances that job is to be the subject governing the verb, no matter how distant that verb may be.

As you saw in the previous chapter, plurals derived from foreign sources, such as *data*, present subject/verb agreement issues. Since these issues occur in all the templates, they will also be found in linking verb templates. Therefore, in a linking verb template using the verb *seem* you have to choose between the following:

The data seems clear.
The data seem clear.

If the second doesn't sit as comfortably in your ear as the first, that is an indication that in everyday usage the singular is becoming established.

Exercises

I. Sentences with Linking Verbs

A. Picking possibilities from each of the slots create ten linking verb sentences. Mix and match as much as you can. Note that in the verb list you have a choice of all the usual linking verbs besides *be*. Do not use a form of *be* more than three times.

Subject	Verb	Subjective Complement
Noun Pronoun Gerund Infinitive	be appear become feel grow look prove remain seem smell stay sound taste turn	Noun Pronoun Adjective

1. _____

2. _____

3. _____

4. _____

5. _____

6. _____

7. _____

8. _____

9. _____

10. _____

Can any of these be turned around so that the resulting sentence would begin with the subjective complement followed by the linking verb and then the subject? If so, which?

B. Create linking template sentences in these patterns, using this key for abbreviations:

N	Noun
P	Pronoun
G	Gerund
I	Infinitive
PP	Prepositional Phrase
ADJ	Adjective
ADV	Adverb
LV	Linking Verb

1. PP   N   LV   ADJ

_____

2. ADV   P   LV   N

_____

3. PP   ADV   PP   N   LV   ADJ

_____

4. N   LV   ADV   ADJ

_____

5. N   LV   ADV   N

_____

6. PP   PP   PP   N   LV   ADJ

_____

7. P   PP   LV   ADJ

_____

8. I   ADV   LV   ADV   ADJ

_____

9. G   LV   ADJ

_____

10. G   LV   N   PP

_____

II. Usage Issues

Pick the formally preferred choice in the following:

1. Susan felt (bad, badly) for the injured dog.
2. Nothing smells so (sweet, sweetly) as a fresh baked pie.
3. Your new idea seems (correct, correctly) for the situation.
4. Henry, among all the applicants in the several batches of candidates, (appear, appears) best suited for the position.
5. It is (I, me) on the phone right now.

III. Recognizing Linking Verb Templates

Which of the following is a linking verb template? Why?

1.
   A. The flowers grow beautiful in the sun.
   B. The flowers grow beautifully in the sun.
2.
   A. The freshly baked pie smells wonderful.
   B. The child smells the freshly baked pie.
3.
   A. The train appeared fast.
   B. The train appeared fast around the bend.
4.
   A. The new bookkeeper looked fastidious.
   B. The new bookkeeper looked fastidiously at the figures.
5.
   A. The situation remains dangerous.
   B. The situation remains in the background of our attention.

CHAPTER FOUR

The Transitive Template I: Direct Objects

We turn now to the transitive verb template, and we shall see that it is a good deal more complicated than the two we have thus far described. As with the other templates, we begin with this one's necessary slots, but we will also deal with the concept of active and passive **voice**.

The Nature of Objects

Traditional grammars explain that in transitive verb structures, the verb "transfers" the action from the subject to another party, termed the "object." We have already seen that latter term when encountering objects of prepositions and verbals. As with so many grammatical terms, *object* derives from a Latin word, in this case literally meaning "thrown against." It is questionable whether that etymology helps explain what the word means in English grammar, other than to suggest its position as the recipient of the action in a transitive verb template. A little more instructive in the traditional definition is the idea of the subject's action having a direct effect on the object, or receiver, of that action.

In a sentence such as the following, the idea of a transfer of action from subject to object makes sense:

The dog bit the man.

Here the action of biting does seem to transfer from the dog to the man. However, in a sentence such as "I understand the problem," the notion does not seem as applicable. That is probably because in this sentence there is no physical "action" to be transferred, unlike in the case of biting. Understanding is still an action of sorts, but it is a mental one rather than physical.

Another way to look at the components of this template is in terms of grammatical relationships. We have already established that the terms *subject* and *verb* have meaning insofar as we recognize that each is tied grammatically to the other (see p. 23). When we talk about objects, we can use the same reasoning, although we are dealing with several variations. Previously, you have seen nouns and noun equivalents as objects of prepositions, as well as of gerunds and infinitives. It is the fact that gerunds and infinitives are derived from verbs that enables them to take objects. Let's look at a few simple examples, first using the noun *book* as an object:

Noun object of a verb:	Jack <u>read</u> the book.
Noun object of an infinitive:	<u>To read</u> a book is a pleasure.
Noun object of a gerund:	<u>Reading</u> a book is a pleasure.

We can substitute the pronoun *it* for the noun phrase containing *book* in each of the above sentences:

Pronoun object of a verb:	Jack read <u>it</u>.
Pronoun object of an infinitive:	To read <u>it</u> is a pleasure
Pronoun object of a gerund:	Reading <u>it</u> is a pleasure.

The Basic Template

Now that we are dealing with the transitive template, we will concentrate on the objects of verbs themselves, not of verbals. Here, then, is the template without any optional slots:

Subject	Verb	Object
Noun Pronoun Gerund Infinitive		Noun Pronoun Gerund Infinitive

Notice two things about this display of the transitive verb template. First, the choices for subject and object are exactly the same, and that is because both demand a noun or noun equivalent. Second, the slot for the verb is left blank because, unlike the linking verb possibilities in the previous chapter, which were limited to a small list of verbs, the choices in this template include almost all the verbs in the English language.

What makes a verb transitive, then, is not the verb itself; rather, it is the verb's grammatical relationship to its object. Without an object, a verb cannot be transitive. With an object, a verb is transitive. Thus, the same verb can often be either intransitive (without an object) or transitive (with an object):

Intransitive: Every morning, Jack <u>walks</u> on the beach.
Transitive: Every morning, Jack <u>walks his dog</u> on the beach.

In the second sentence, *his dog* is the object of *walks*. Both sentences conclude with the prepositional phrase "on the beach" in an optional slot functioning as an adverb.

Intransitive: My daughter <u>reads</u> very well.
Transitive: My daughter <u>reads</u> that book very well.

And, finally, some verbs can be intransitive, but linking when they have a subjective complement, and transitive when they have an object:

Intransitive: Every day the kitten <u>grows</u>.
Linking: The kitten <u>grows</u> fat.
Transitive: The kitten cannot <u>grow</u> flowers.

Voice

Transitive verb templates are expressed in either the **active** or **passive voice**. All of the discussion above dealt with the template in the active voice. In this case, the terminology of *active* and *passive* is helpful, since in the transitive verb template, an action is expressed. When the action moves from the subject to the object, it makes sense to say that the subject is being active. And if the situation is reversed such that the subject is being acted upon, it also is reasonable to say that the subject is being passive. Here is an illustration:

Active: The dog bit the man.
Passive: The man was bitten by the dog.

Notice what happens grammatically in the switch from active to passive voice. First, the subject changes. And remember, by the subject we mean the noun, or noun equivalent, that governs a particular verb, in this case the verb *bite*. In the active voice, the subject is *the dog* while in the passive alternative it is *the man*. And, again, this makes sense as the dog is doing the action, or being active, while the man is being acted upon in a passive sense. In the passive version, the noun that was the subject of the active voice occurs in another slot as the object of the preposition *by*;

it is often termed the agent, since it is responsible for the action of the verb. In the sentence above, the active voice subject *dog* becomes the agent in the passive when it is the object of *by*.

As it turns out, we can call this slot optional because it is possible, and in fact not unusual, to write a sentence in the passive voice without it:

> With the slot: The man was bitten <u>by the dog</u>.
> Without the slot: The man was bitten.

Composing passive voice sentences without this optional slot can lead to some interesting confusion, as you will see later in this chapter (pp. 67–68).

Besides adding this optional slot, the passive voice also requires a different form of the verb. In the active voice in our example, the verb was a one-word past tense: *bit*. In the passive voice construction, however, the verb, still in the past tense, is a **verb phrase**. Verb phrases contain an **auxiliary**, or helping, verb (and sometimes more than one), and they end with a form of the main verb. In this case, the auxiliary verb is *was* (the past form of *be*), and the main verb is *bitten*, which is the **past participle** of *bite*. The verb phrase in a passive voice sentence always contains a form of *be* as the auxiliary, in the same tense as the verb in the active voice, followed by the past participle of the main verb. The past participle of any verb can be discovered by asking what form of the main verb would be placed in this sentence:

> I have_____.

The verb form that you would put in the blank is its past participle. For regular verbs, the past participle is the same as the past tense of the verb. Both simply add an *-ed* suffix. Applying that principle to our illustration above for the regular verb *walk* produces the following:

> I have walked.

Walked is thus the past participle of *walk*. English, however, has many irregular verbs, and *bite* is one of them. Others include *drink* (past participle: *drunk*), *bring* (past participle: *brought*), and *go* (past participle: *gone*).

Just as we saw with present participles, a past participle can also be used as an adjective modifier:

> The <u>bitten</u> man went to the emergency room.

This duality of function, combined with the possibility of dropping the optional **by phrase** in passive voice sentences leads to the confusions mentioned above.

With all of the above in mind, we can look at the transitive verb template in the passive voice:

Subject	Verb Phrase	Optional *by* Phrase
Noun Pronoun Gerund Infinitive	Form of *be* + past participle Form of *get* + past participle	*by* + active voice subject

You probably notice that this version of the template contains more specific requirements in the verb and optional slot; that is simply because those requirements are necessary for the expression of the passive voice. In addition, the much more informal *get* has been added to the verb slot, as it is possible to use it in place of the verb *be*:

The unwary pedestrian <u>was hit</u> by the bus.

can be expressed with the *get* form:

The unwary pedestrian <u>got hit</u> by the bus.

For the sake of simplicity, you will see only the more formal version (using *be*) in subsequent examples.

Expanding the Transitive Verb Template

Like all templates, the transitive verb template can be expanded by adding optional slots. For example, as always, we can add optional slots before the subject. Let's start by defining these abbreviations, before using them to build a transitive verb template:

S	Subject
V	Verb
O	Object
PP	Prepositional Phrase
ADV	Adverb
NP	Noun Phrase

S	V	O
Jack	belted	a home run.

Add a prepositional phrase before the subject:

PP	**S**	**V**	**O**
In the ninth inning,	Jack	belted	a home run.

Put a prepositional phrase after the object:

PP	**S**	**V**	**O**	**PP**
In the ninth inning,	Jack	belted	a home run	over the fence.

Put an adverb before the verb:

PP	**S**	**Adv**	**V**	**O**	**PP**
In the ninth inning,	Jack	unexpectedly	belted	a home run	over the fence.

Let's put one more prepositional phrase at the end of the sentence:

PP	**S**	**Adv**	**V**	**O**	**PP**
In the ninth inning,	Jack	unexpectedly	belted	a home run	over the fence

PP
for the winning hit.

Finally, let's insert a noun phrase in apposition, functioning as an adjective modifying the subject. You already know that a noun phrase is a constituent consisting of a noun as the head of the phrase preceded by adjectives and/or noun determiners. For this example, we will construct a noun phrase with *hitter*, preceded by the noun determiner *a* and the adjective *poor*: *a poor hitter*.

Our fully expanded sentence now reads this way:

S	**NP**	**Adv**	**V**	**O**	**PP**
Jack,	a poor hitter,	unexpectedly	belted	a home run	over the fence

PP
for the winning run.

Now let's put this into the passive voice, starting with the simple sentence without the added optional slots.

Active Voice:	Jack belted a home run
Passive Voice:	A home run was belted by Jack.

Things become a little complicated as we add the optional slots, so we will do them one at a time. We can leave the first prepositional phrase as the beginning of the sentence. It is an adverb, and as such, its position is variable.

PP   **S**   **V**   **PP** *(by)*
In the ninth inning, a home run was belted by Jack.

Or we can put it at the end of the sentence:

A home run was belted by Jack in the ninth inning.

You can probably see that other positions in the sentence are also possible.
Now let's add the prepositional phrase *over the fence*:

PP   **S**   **V**   **PP**   **PP** *(by)*
In the ninth inning, a home run was belted over the fence by Jack.

In this case, the prepositional phrase has to follow the verb. Placing it after the *by* phrase would result with something that sounds awkward:

In the ninth inning, a home run was belted by Jack over the fence.

That reads as though Jack were over the fence, not the baseball he hit.
Now add the adverb:

PP   **S**   **Adv**   **V**   **PP**   **PP** *(by)*
In the ninth inning, a home run unexpectedly was belted over the fence by Jack.

Again, the adverb "unexpectedly" can be moved around. We'll finish by inserting the noun phrase in apposition:

PP	**S**	**Adv**	**V**	**PP**
In the ninth inning,	a home run	unexpectedly	was belted	over the fence

PP *(by)*	**NP**
by Jack,	a poor hitter.

This example leads naturally into the main stylistic issue for the transitive verb template.

Matters of Style

Choosing Active or Passive

As you have seen, the same idea can be expressed in the transitive verb template in either the active or the passive voice. Grammatically, both are acceptable. However, thinking in terms of style usually leads toward a preference for the active voice, except in those circumstances where the doer of the action is less important than the action itself.

Let's examine the choice between active and passive for the illustrative sentences above. There are two main facts being expressed in those sentences: a home run won the game, and Jack hit that home run. Here is the sentence using the active voice and including the important information expressed in the appositive phrase:

Jack, a weak hitter, belted a home run.

Stylistically, the main point to be made is that a weak hitter belted a home run.

Now, let's see how the emphasis shifts when the sentence is expressed using the passive voice:

A home run was belted by Jack, a weak hitter.

In this passive version, weak-hitting Jack is reduced to the agent role, the object of a prepositional phrase. That is what the passive does: it reduces the subject of the active voice into a phrase that reads as little more than an afterthought.

There are times, however, when the passive voice can be a better choice for stylistic reasons. In these instances, the doer of the action is not important, or may not even be known, as in the following:

The public library in our town was built a century ago.

The important piece of information in this sentence is when the library was built—in other words, that it is a century-old structure—and not who built it. In fact, it is likely that it would take some research to discover who the builder was. Even if you wanted to extend the idea beyond the actual builder to the organization that authorized the construction, you would likely come up with an uninteresting fact, such as the town council, or the county board of commissioners.

On the other hand, the builder or founder of an institution can sometimes be as important as, or even more important than, the institution itself:

Thomas Jefferson founded the University of Virginia.

That idea is expressed in the active voice. Switching it to the passive would diminish the significance of Jefferson while boosting the importance of the university:

> The University of Virginia was founded by Thomas Jefferson.

Perhaps this passive-voice construction would be appropriate in promotional material put out by the university, because the material is aimed at people—such as parents and potential students—who are interested in the university. The fact that Jefferson founded it would no doubt be of interest, and probably a plus, but not what the target audience was most concerned about.

As a question of effective style, the active voice is crisper and more emphatic, while the passive voice tends to be wordier and, as its very name suggests, less direct. However, the passive voice is useful in situations where the doer of the action is less important than the action itself. This quality is emphasized by the ease with which the *by* phrase of the passive can be eliminated so that the doer of the action literally disappears from the statement.

Possible Ambiguity in the Passive Voice

As noted above (p. 62), the passive-voice verb phrase includes a form of *be* followed by the past participle. Because a past participle can also function as an adjective, and because *be* is the most common linking verb, this combination is perfectly ambiguous in grammatical terms. As a result, readers often have no way of knowing from the grammatical structure alone whether the combination of *be* plus the past participle is part of a linking verb template or whether it is the verb phrase of the passive voice in a transitive template:

> They were delighted.

Readers encountering this sentence would not be sure whether the sentence was in a linking verb or a passive voice template. Adding the *by* phrase for the passive voice version eliminates the confusion:

> They were delighted by the news.

Although context or the inclusion of the *by* phrase eliminates the ambiguity, you as a writer should recognize that the confusion will occur. As a stylistic matter, you have to decide whether that momentary confusion creates the intended effect on your audience or whether it should be avoided. The choice between immediate clarity or brief uncertainty followed by clarification is a question of style.

For an example of intentional ambiguity, look at this slogan from some years back by automobile manufacturer Datsun:

We are driven.

Here the advertising slogan gets a two-for-one impact because of its grammatical ambiguity. The word *driven* is the past participle of *drive*. As such, it can occur either as an adjective in a linking verb template, or as part of the verb phrase in a passive voice template.

In the linking verb template possibility, *driven* would mean something like "highly motivated" to do something, and it would be an adjective modifier of the subject *we*. Thus, since this slogan advertises an automobile manufacturer, this little three-word sentence would suggest that the company was highly motivated to do the best it could in producing automobiles.

In the passive voice alternative, on the other hand, the slogan can either mean something similar or something quite different. If we keep the same meaning of *driven* as it has in the linking verb template, and add a *by* phrase, the result is very much like the linking verb version:

We are driven by the desire for the highest quality.

That can, of course, be expressed in the active voice:

The desire for the highest quality drives us.

But with a different *by* phrase, the slogan takes on an entirely new meaning:

We are driven by thousands of satisfied customers.

Here the point is that because the automobile is so good, many, many people can be found driving it.

Whenever the adjectival meaning of a past participle and its passive verb phrase meaning are not the same, and the *by* phrase is omitted in the passive construction, the sentence will be ambiguous, with two possible meanings. If this ambiguity is intentional, as it is in the above example, it represents an informed stylistic choice. If it is unintentional, and leaves the reader uncertain as to what meaning is intended, it is a stylistic mistake that should be eliminated. The active voice, of course, does not lead to ambiguities such as these.

Matters of Usage

The familiar problems of subject-verb agreement, and adjective/adverb issues occur in the transitive verb template, so a few examples should suffice.

Subject-Verb Agreement

Consider this sentence:

> Jill with her friends throw a party every Friday night.

The problem in this transitive verb template is disagreement between the subject Jill and the verb *throw*. What causes the issue is the plural object of the prepositional phrase "with her friends." Because that plural noun immediately precedes the verb, the temptation is to have the verb agree with it. However, the syntactic rule that each constituent in a sentence can perform only one job, along with its corollary that each constituent must be doing something, prevents *friends* from being both an object of the preposition and the subject of the verb; the rule also gives the noun *Jill* something to do, namely function as the subject of the verb *throw*. These considerations produce this preferable version of the sentence:

> Jill with her friends throws a party every Friday night.

Notice, however, that if the preposition *with* is replaced by the **conjunction** *and*, there is a different grammatical situation. In that case, the sentence now has a compound subject because there no longer is a prepositional phrase, and that compound subject requires a plural verb:

> Jill and her friends throw a party every Friday night.

Adjectives and Adverbs

In terms of the second common usage problem, verbs in both intransitive and transitive templates should be modified by adverbs, not adjectives:

> The team's new guard shoots the three point shot easy.

Here *easy* is separated from the verb it modifies, but it still should be in the adverb form:

> The team's new guard shoots the three point shot easily.

Note that placing the word next to the verb clearly indicates which possibility is grammatically preferable:

> The team's new guard easily shoots the three point shot.

That probably sounds fine to your ear. But putting the adjective in that same position produces a much less desirable (and much less accurate) sentence:

> The team's new guard easy shoots the three point shot.

Pronoun Case

A usage issue particular to the transitive verb template is the case of a pronoun in the object slot. Because English nouns do not show case, this issue does not occur with them, but it does surface when an object is a pronoun:

> The principal congratulated <u>Jack and I</u> for our perfect attendance.

This is another instance of hypercorrectness: we have been told so many times that the subjective form *I* is preferable to the objective form *me* that we are tempted to use the *I* form where it does not belong, as in the sentence above.

Changing the order of the two objects so that the pronoun comes first emphasizes how inappropriate the subjective pronoun is in the object slot:

> The principal congratulated <u>I and Jack</u> for our perfect attendance.

Putting the preferred form *me* in that slot sounds a lot better:

> The principal congratulated <u>me and Jack</u> for our perfect attendance.

Whether it is preferable to place the reference to yourself after the other person is a question of manners, not grammar. Both "congratulated me and Jack" and "congratulated Jack and me" are equally acceptable as a question of grammar.

This same problem of hyper correctness regularly occurs when there are two objects of a preposition, one of which is a pronoun:

> The principal called <u>for Jack and I</u> to receive our awards.
> The principal called <u>for Jack and me</u> to receive our awards.

The same test as used above for two objects of a verb should lead you to prefer the second choice using *me* rather than *I*. By the same logic, the phrase "between you and me" is preferable to the hypercorrected "between you and I."

This issue will show up again in the next chapter, where the objects in question are indirect rather than direct.

Special Cases in Transitive/Intransitive Templates

English confounds its users with a few special cases where the form of the verb changes depending upon whether it occurs in a transitive or an intransitive template. Chief among these troublesome instances is the *lie/lay* combination.

First, we have to understand that forms of *lie* are preferred in intransitive templates while forms of *lay* are preferred in transitive templates. Said another way, the choice between these two depends upon whether the verb has no object (*lie*) or does have an object (*lay*).

To add to the confusion, the forms of these two verbs overlap as you can see in Table 4.1:

TABLE 4.1: *LAY VS. LIE*

	Infinitive	Past	Past Participle	Present Participle
Intransitive	lie	lay	lain	lying
Transitive	lay	laid	laid	laying

As the table indicates, the past of *lie* is the same as the infinitive form of *lay*. Notice as well that the forms of *lie* are irregular with the vowel change and the *-n* suffix on the past participle. On the other hand, the forms of *lay* are basically regular, since a *-d* suffix is really the same as the regular *-ed* suffix used to form the past tense and past participle. In all of this confusion of form, at least the present participle of each is the regular *-ing* form. Unfortunately, however, *lying* is also the present participle of the regular verb *lie*, which means to tell an untruth.

Users of English who want to select the preferred form have first to decide whether the template in which these words are to be inserted is intransitive or transitive and then, having made that decision, must remember the right form. In any event, here are some examples of the preferred choices:

Intransitive:　Jill <u>lay</u> down for a nap an hour ago.

In this sentence, *lay* is the past tense of *lie* in an intransitive template.

> Transitive: Jack <u>laid</u> the glass carefully on the table.

In this one, *laid* is the past tense of *lay* in a transitive sentence.

> Intransitive: Jill was <u>lying</u> on the beach all afternoon.

Here, *lying* is the present participle of *lie* in an intransitive template.

> Transitive: Jack's chickens <u>are laying</u> dozens of eggs.

This one has the present participle of *lay* in the verb phrase of a transitive template.

   These few examples show how difficult it is to find the preferred choice, and this might explain why the irregular forms of *lie* are infrequently heard in everyday English. Yet, in formal circumstances, they are still expected.

   A similar distinction, though less confusing in terms of form, is found in the uses of *shine*. The forms of this verb are regular in transitive verb templates but irregular in intransitive ones:

> Intransitive: The sun shone (or has shone) through the clouds.
> Transitive: Jack shined (or has shined) his shoes before the prom.

Because the form differences are easier to deal with, this pair presents less of a challenge.

Exercises

I. Sentences with Transitive Verbs

A. Picking possibilities from each of the slots, create ten transitive verb sentences. Mix and match as much as you can. Note that some of the verbs in the list also appeared as linking verbs, so be careful to make sure that they are followed by an object, not a subjective complement. Use each verb only once.

Subject	Verb	Object
Noun Pronoun Gerund Infinitive	bite like become feel grow read build start elect smell	Noun Pronoun Gerund Infinitive

1. _____

2. _____

3. _____

4. _____

5. _____

6. _____

7. _____

8. _____

9. _____

10. _____

B. Now turn five of your sentences into the passive voice. Write the sentence first with the *by* phrase, and then without it.

1. _____

_____

2. _____

_____

3. _____

_____

4. _____

_____

5. _____

_____

C. Create active voice transitive template sentences in the patterns indicated, using this key for abbreviations:

N	Noun
P	Pronoun
G	Gerund
I	Infinitive
PP	Prepositional Phrase
ADJ	Adjective
ADV	Adverb
ATV	Active Transitive Verb

1. G   ATV   G

_____

2. PP   N   ATV   P   PP

_____

3. P   ATV   I   PP

_____

4. PP   ADJ   N   ATV   G   PP

_____

5. ADV   P   ATV   NP   PP

_____

D. Create passive voice transitive template sentences in the patterns indicated, using this key for abbreviations:

N	Noun
P	Pronoun
PP	Prepositional Phrase
ADJ	Adjective
ADV	Adverb
PTV	Passive Transitive Verb
B	*By* phrase

1. P   PTV   B

_____

2. N   PTV   B

_____

3. PP   P   PTV   ADV   B

_____

4. ADV   N   PTV   PP

_____

5. N   and   P   PTV   B

_____

II. *Usage Matters*

A. Pick the formally preferred choice in the following:

1. Jack and his friends (studies, study) the test material every day.
2. Jill styles hair (good, well).
3. Jack as well as Jill (drives, drive) new cars.
4. In the ninth inning one of the players (was, were) thrown out of the game by the umpire.
5. Jill greeted my brother and (me, I) at the door of the party.

B. Pick the formally preferred choice in the following.

1. Now I (lay, lie) me down to sleep.
2. After a while, Jack saw his book (lying, laying) on the table.
3. The morning sun (shined, shone) through Jill's bedroom window.
4. Jack (shined, shone) the hubcaps of his new car.
5. Jack and Jill had (lain, laid) their burden down.

III. *Past Participles*

Try to think of a pair of sentences using a past participle in an ambiguous way where the grammar does not indicate whether the template is a linking verb or a transitive in the passive voice template. Look at the Datsun example (p. 68) for a model.

CHAPTER FIVE

The Transitive Template II: Indirect Objects

In the last chapter, you saw the basic transitive verb template in both the active and the passive voice. In this chapter and the next, you will see that transitive verb templates can also occur with two other variations: those with indirect as well as direct objects, and those with objective complements.

Indirect Objects

Traditional grammar, based on meaning, would say that an indirect object is the recipient of the direct object:

> Jill gave a bone to her dog.

Here *dog* is the indirect object while *bone* is the direct object. The terminology makes some sense, because Jill did something with the bone, so the bone is directly connected to Jill's action. And, then, her dog received the bone. Perhaps switching these two makes the point clearer:

> Jill gave her dog to a bone.

Although this version is nonsensical, it does suggest the reason for the terminology. The syntax of this sentence would have us believe that Jill made a gift of her dog, and gave that gift to a bone. Worded this way, *dog* is the direct object, and *bone* is the indirect object. If we change the sentence one more time to make it more meaningful, we will see the terminology at work even better. Let's keep *dog* as the direct object, but let's provide a different indirect object:

Jill gave her dog to Jack.

Here we see that Jill's action is first connected to the direct object, *dog*, while the indirect object *Jack* receives that direct object.

However useful this traditional way of looking at indirect objects may be, it is important to stress that the only way for there to be an indirect object in the transitive verb template is for it to be in combination with a direct object, such as we have already described, and a verb that permits both kinds of object. Furthermore, the combination of direct and indirect objects in the transitive verb template occurs in two different syntactic patterns.

In the examples above, the indirect objects follow the direct objects and appear in what seem to be prepositional phrases: *to her dog*, or *to Jack*. In fact, some grammarians would insist that in this position, these are not indirect objects but rather objects of the preposition. We, however, will continue to call them indirect objects for the very good reason that when we look at the second syntactic pattern we see that the preposition can be eliminated:

Jill gave her dog a bone.
Jill gave Jack her dog.

In these alternatives, the indirect object comes first, followed by the direct object, and there is no need for a preposition. Therefore, whether the indirect object follows the direct object and is preceded by *for* or *to*, or whether it precedes the direct object without an introductory word, the sentence communicates exactly the same thing.

Here are some more examples, expressed both ways:

The teacher gave us an assignment.
The teacher gave an assignment to us.
The car salesman made Jack a deal.
The car salesman made a deal for Jack.
Jill loaned her brother money.
Jill loaned money to her bother.
Jack and Jill offered their friends a laptop.
Jack and Jill offered a laptop to their friends.

The Basic Templates

All of these examples are in the active voice, and the templates are as follows:

Subject	Verb	Indirect Object	Direct Object
Noun Pronoun Gerund Infinitive		Noun Pronoun	Noun Pronoun

Subject	Verb	Direct Object		Indirect Object
Noun Pronoun Gerund Infinitive		Noun Pronoun	to for	Noun Pronoun Gerund

Note that gerunds and infinitives, the verbal noun equivalents, have been left out of object slots. It is possible to compose a sentence using a verbal subject:

> Eating too much cake gave Jack a stomachache.

Verbals do not occur in the direct object slots, but gerunds sometimes appear as indirect objects:

> The great prize gave even more appeal to winning the contest.
> The great prize gave winning the contest even more appeal.

Worded either way, the indirect object using the gerund *winning* with its object *the contest* sounds fine.

Expanding the Templates

These templates can be expanded, as you have seen before, by adding optional slots as well as modifiers within the slots. For example, let's work with the sample sentence from the beginning of the chapter. The abbreviations DO and IO stand for direct and indirect objects, respectively.

S V   DO   IO
Jill gave a bone to her dog.

Add an adverbial prepositional phrase to the start of the sentence:

PP   S V   DO   IO
After her dinner, Jill gave a bone to her dog.

Now let's add a prepositional phrase after the object:

PP   S V   DO PP   IO
After her dinner, Jill gave a bone from her steak to her dog.

How about a noun in apposition after the subject:

PP   S NP   V   DO PP   IO
After her dinner, Jill, a dedicated pet owner, gave a bone from her steak to her dog.

And finally, let's insert another prepositional phrase after the object:

PP   S   NP   V   DO   PP
After her dinner, Jill,   a dedicated pet owner, gave a bone from her steak
PP   IO
still on her plate to her dog.

Here's how this expanded sentence looks in the alternative pattern for this template with the indirect object coming first:

PP   S   NP   V   IO   DO
After her dinner, Jill,   a dedicated pet owner, gave her dog a bone
PP   PP
from her steak   still on her plate.

As a matter of style, as you will see in the next section, this alternative version seems a little bit tighter. On the other hand, it loses the tension of the version where the indirect object comes at the very end of the sentence.

Let's expand the template containing a verbal subject, starting with the example sentence from earlier:

Eating too much cake gave Jack a stomachache.

Add a prepositional phrase:

> At his birthday party, eating too much cake gave Jack a stomachache.

Now insert an adverb before the verb:

> At his birthday party, eating too much cake predictably
> gave Jack a stomachache.

Finally, one more prepositional phrase at the end of the sentence after the direct object:

> At his birthday party, eating too much cake predictably gave Jack a
> stomachache of major proportions.

Although infinitives can also serve in the subject slot, the results are not very pleasing:

> To eat too much cake will give you a stomachache.
> At your party, to eat too much cake will give you a stomachache.
> At your party, to eat too much cake predictably will give you a stomachache.
> At your party, to eat too much cake predictably will give you a
> stomachache of major proportions.

Matters of Style

Creating tension is one of the most effective ways to have your sentences work for you. Most readers anticipate as they work their way through a sentence. This process involves recognizing the syntax of the unfolding sentence, as well as checking the content against known and remembered ideas. As a careful writer, you can make this reader anticipation work for you.

Consider how the verb *give* creates anticipation in the reader. That verb almost never appears without an object. Therefore, when readers encounter a form of *give*, they wait to find out what was given, which would be the direct object. They think, reasonably, that the subject of the sentence must have given something. Once they know what was given, they probably wait to find out to whom it was given, and that would be the indirect object.

Let's see how anticipation can work in this template. Here is the beginning of a sentence:

> Jill gave . . .

As you begin to read any sentence, you tune in to both content and syntactic form. The notion of "content" suggests an understanding of the words themselves, not just what they mean in a dictionary sense, but what we already know, if anything, about them. For example, if the first noun in the subject slot of a sentence is *house*, you likely form a quick mental image of the houses that are most prominently stored in your memory. In the case of a proper noun, such as *Jill*, you search your memory for people with that name.

Because context helps you locate the Jills you have stored in your memory, let's provide a little context for our sentence, and suggest that it occurs in a continuation of the Jack and Jill story. In that case, reading *Jill*'s name and then the verb *gave* would probably cause you to guess, i.e., anticipate, that whatever Jill gave, she gave it to Jack. You would also be aware of what you already know about this couple, namely, that they went up a hill searching for water and experienced an unfortunate accident that left Jack with a serious, but perhaps not fatal, injury. Jill seems to have emerged in better shape from the accident.

So what might Jill have given to Jack? Here is where the choice this template provides between placement of the two objects becomes a stylistic issue. If the writer wants to create maximum tension, the idea would be to leave the unknown, or lesser known, piece of information to the very end of the sentence, so the reader will be drawn toward the sentence's conclusion. Since we are suggesting that readers would guess that Jack most likely would be the indirect object, the remaining uncertainty is the direct object, namely, what Jill gave to Jack. Therefore, the pattern that would best withhold this information to the end of the sentence is the one where the indirect object comes first:

Jill gave Jack a_____.

The gap indicates the as-yet-undeclared direct object, the thing that Jill gave to Jack. Continuing with the idea that this sentence occurs in the Jack and Jill story after Jack broke his crown, perhaps this sentence would make sense:

Jill gave Jack a get-well card.

Now let's make this part of the story more interesting by adding what narrative writers call the "back story," which is a past action or situation that sheds light on the present. In this case, let's say that Jack has a habit of carelessly running up the hill in his search for water, and has fallen down more than once before. As the writer, you would know that your readers would be unaware of this piece of back story because you have just made it up, and you would want to express it with maximum effect.

Thus you would start the sentence this way:

Jill gave Jack...

Your reader would expect you to say that Jill gave Jack something nice. After all, he is lying there in his hospital bed with a dented skull. But instead, you write the following:

Jill gave Jack a lecture about his careless running up the hill.

With *lecture* now as the direct object, followed by the prepositional phrase that suggests the back story, the sentence would have a strong effect. It begins with the expected, that Jill gave Jack something, but concludes with the unexpected, a lecture on carelessness rather than the more likely get-well card.

Matters of Usage

We encounter usage issues in this template similar to those discussed in the previous chapter on transitive verbs, as well as elsewhere.

Pronoun Case

As you will recall from the previous chapter, pronouns in English change their form to reflect whether they are functioning as subjects or objects. And since this template involves objects, the usage issue of pronoun case will arise with some frequency:

Our professor gave Jill and (I, me) extra credit on our assignment.

Here the direct object *extra credit* comes after the indirect object *Jill and (I, me)*. It is important to remember that the indirect object is still an object, so any pronoun that occurs as part of the indirect object slot should be in the objective case rather than the subjective:

Our professor gave Jill and <u>me</u> extra credit on our assignment.

Writing the sentence in the alternative pattern of direct object first followed by the indirect object introduced by *to* produces the following:

Our professor gave extra credit on our assignment to Jill and <u>me</u>.

It is possible that in this position, where the indirect object is farther removed from the verb, there might be a stronger tendency to use the subjective form of the pronoun. On the other hand, the introductory word *to* makes what follows feel like a prepositional phrase, so that should reinforce the choice of the objective case pronoun.

Let's look at one more example of this usage issue. Compare the following:

> Jill's uncle offered a business opportunity to Jack and (her, she).
> Jill's uncle offered Jack and (her, she) a business opportunity.

In both variations, the preferred choice, as you will have guessed, is the objective *her*. You might also note that these usage issues arise when there are **compound objects**. It is highly unlikely that if you took *Jack* out of these sentences you would choose *she*:

> Jill's uncle offered she a business opportunity.
> Jill's uncle offered a business opportunity to she.

Both of those should sound obviously wrong. However, a compound object starting with a noun such as *Jack* clearly seems right, so the pronoun then becomes vulnerable to the mistake of hypercorrectness discussed above (p. 52, 70).

Subject-Verb Agreement

This usage issue, as you have seen, crops up in every template, occurring usually when the object of a prepositional phrase that is modifying the subject is grammatically different from that subject and seems to govern the verb, as in the following:

> Jill with her friends give their church a cake for its sale.
> Jill with her friends gives their church a weekly donation.

If you see the prepositional phrase *with her friends*, you can avoid being distracted both by its plural object *friends*, as well as by the plural *their* after the verb, and correctly see that *Jill* is the singular subject of the verb, so that the second choice above is preferred. Phrasing the sentence in the alternative pattern would then read as follows:

> Jill with her friends gives a weekly donation to their church.

Let's take a look at an example featuring Jack:

Jack together with his teammates give their opponents a tough game.
Jack together with his teammates gives their opponents a tough game.

The same reasoning as the Jill example applies here, so the preferred choice has *Jack* as the singular subject governing the singular verb *gives:*

Jack together with his teammates gives their opponents a tough game.

Or in the alternative pattern for this template:

Jack together with his teammates gives a tough game to their opponents.

In both examples, beginning the sentence with the prepositional phrase makes the preferred choice quite clear:

With her friends, Jill gives a weekly donation to their church.
With her friends, Jill gives their church a weekly donation.
With his teammates, Jack gives their opponents a tough game.
With his teammates, Jack gives a tough game to their opponents.

Note that stylistically, both the Jill sentences read equally well, but of the two Jack sentences, the first version, which has the indirect object first, reads better than the one that has the direct object first, perhaps because "giving a game" is more figurative than the literal "giving a donation."

Exercises

I. Sentences with Indirect Objects

A. Using the verb *give*, and choosing among the possibilities in the other slots, compose ten sentences in this pattern:

Subject	**Verb**	**Indirect Object**	**Direct Object**
Noun Pronoun Gerund Infinitive	give	Noun Pronoun	Noun Pronoun

1. _____
2. _____
3. _____
4. _____
5. _____
6. _____
7. _____
8. _____
9. _____
10. _____

B. Now change your sentences into this alternative pattern:

Subject	**Verb**	**Direct Object**		**Indirect Object**
Noun Pronoun Gerund Infinitive	give	Noun Pronoun	to for	Noun Pronoun

1. _____

2. _____

3. _____

4. _____

5. _____

6. _____

7. _____

8. _____

9. _____

10. _____

C. Create direct/indirect object transitive template sentences in these patterns, using this key for abbreviations:

N	Noun
P	Pronoun
G	Gerund
I	Infinitive
V	Verb
PP	Prepositional Phrase
ADJ	Adjective
ADV	Adverb
DO	Direct Object
IO	Indirect Object

1. ADV   P   V   ADJ   DO   IO

_____

2. PP   N   ADV   V   IO   DO

_____

3. G   N   PP   V   IO   DO

_____

4. ADJ   N   ADV   V   IO   DO

_____

5. PP   PP   P   V   ADJ   DO   IO

_____

II. Usage Matters

The sentences below have either subject/verb or pronoun case usage issues. Pick the preferred choice in the parentheses for each sentence.

1. The club and its members (give, gives) time to the community.
2. Our coach gave Jack and (I, me) the new game plan.
3. All the students in the class except me (give, gives) the substitute teacher a hard time.
4. The car salesman gave a good price on the used car to Jill and (I, me).
5. Everyone shows Jack, Jill, and (I, me) full respect.

CHAPTER SIX

The Transitive Template III: Objective Complements

This template is one more variation of the basic transitive verb complement. Previously, you saw that template includes a transitive verb and its direct object, and that the first variation of this template added an indirect object to go along with the direct object. In the present chapter, you will see that transitive verbs can also have an objective complement.

Objective Complements

In this template, a complement completes the meaning of the direct object, just as a subjective complement completes the meaning of the subject in the linking verb template:

> Subjective Complement: Jack is <u>the class president</u>.
> Objective Complement: The class elected Jack <u>president</u>.

Here the complement in both sentences is the noun *president*. As is the case in linking verb templates, the complement can also be an adjective:

> Subjective Complement: Jill is <u>intelligent</u>.
> Objective Complement: Jack considers Jill <u>intelligent</u>.

Notice that the verbs in these examples are different because the templates in which they occur require different verbs. In the linking verb versions, the verb is the common linking verb *be*, while in the objective complement sentence the verbs are the transitive *elected* and *considers*.

The parallel between subjective and objective complements can be seen clearly by creating a linking verb template out of the relationship between the object and the objective complement. This is accomplished simply by inserting a linking verb between the object and the objective complement. See how this works with the example sentences above:

	Object		**Objective Complement**
The class elected	Jack	(is)	president.
Jack considers	Jill	(is)	intelligent.

Another way of expressing this sentence is to insert "to be" between the object and the complement:

The class elected Jack to be president.

Jack considers Jill to be intelligent.

This variation sounds perfectly fine, and the infinitive phrase emphasizes the comparison with the linking verb template.

The Basic Template

We can now lay out the objective complement template:

Subject	**Verb**	**Direct Object**	**Objective Complement**	
Noun Pronoun Gerund Infinitive		Noun Pronoun Gerund	(to be)	Noun Adjective

Notice that the slot in the template for the objective complement lacks the pronoun possibility found in the linking verb template's subjective complement, because it is unlikely to find a pronoun in that spot in this template. Notice as well that while it is possible to have a gerund noun equivalent in the direct object slot an infinitive does not work as well:

Jack considers swimming great exercise.

The gerund *swimming* as direct object sounds fine. However, the infinitive *to swim* in the same position does not:

> Jack considers to swim great exercise.

Arguably this sentence still sounds like English, but of a forced or strained type.

Expanding the Template

As you have seen in the previous chapters, the transitive template is generally expanded by adding modifiers in optional slots. One common addition in any template is to place a prepositional phrase before the subject. Such a phrase is usually adverbial:

> <u>After consideration</u>, Jack believed his friend truthful.

As before, add a noun in apposition after the subject:

> After consideration, Jack, <u>a careful man</u>, believed his friend truthful.

Now, insert an adverb before the verb:

> After consideration, Jack, a careful man, <u>happily</u> believed his friend truthful.

Next, put a couple of prepositional phrases at the end of the sentence:

> After consideration, Jack, a careful man, happily believed his friend truthful <u>in spite of the evidence to the contrary</u>.

Finally, let's see how the sentence sounds with the *(to be)* alternative:

> After consideration, Jack, a careful man, happily believed his friend to be truthful in spite of the evidence to the contrary.

Let's try another expansion, this time starting with gerunds in the subject and object slots:

> Solving difficult problems made working a challenge.

Notice, as is often the case, the gerund in the subject slot *solving* has its own object *difficult problems*. The sentence, though, sounds a little incomplete even though it is syntactically whole. That deficiency can be fixed by adding an adverbial prepositional phrase after the gerund *working* in the object slot:

> Solving difficult problems made working <u>in the new laboratory</u> a challenge.

As you can see from this example, even though we call prepositional phrases and other modifiers optional additions to a template, they often provide useful, if not crucial, information. Seen from this perspective, you can understand that the term "optional" refers to the minimal syntactic structure of a template, and not the necessary information of the statement. Each template, as you have seen, is the syntactic skeleton required to formulate a grammatically complete thought in English, and just as skeletons usually need to be covered by flesh, templates often need to be fleshed out with "optional" material, as in the sentence above.

Let's fill a couple more optional slots with prepositional phrases:

> For Jill, solving difficult problems under severe time constraints made working in the new laboratory a challenge.

The additional material now connects a particular person *Jill* to the statement, and further defines the nature of the problems as being *under severe time constraints.*

Matters of Style

Tension in this template occurs in quite a similar way to what you saw in the previous chapter. The discussion of the direct/indirect object template indicated how *give*, the verb commonly found in that template, creates anticipation, first by indicating that the subject transfers something (the direct object) and then by defining the recipient of that transfer (the indirect object).

Anticipation is established in the objective complement template in a similar way, but involving a wider variety of verbs. Such verbs as *consider, think, make*, and so forth, often are followed by both an object and an objective complement:

> Jack considers jogging boring.
> Jill thinks it necessary exercise.
> Running with Jill makes jogging tolerable for Jack.

Notice how each of these sentences would sound incomplete without the objective complements:

> Jack considers jogging.
> Jill thinks it.
> Running with Jill makes jogging.

These sentences are syntactically whole and conform to the transitive verb template by containing a verb and an object of the verb. Yet, in spite of that conformity, they seem to be pointing toward something that isn't there. In each case, that something is provided by the objective complement.

Just as with the direct/indirect object template, writers can work with the reader anticipation created in this template in the same way. Let's take a look at the sentences above.

In the first one, readers are told that Jack has an attitude toward jogging, but they do not know what that might be. Consequently, readers come to the direct object anticipating finding out just what Jack thinks about jogging. This is the anticipation the writer can work with. Some readers would guess that Jack has a positive attitude toward jogging, since that is a widely held view:

> Jack considers jogging <u>beneficial</u>.

That sentence answers the question raised by the structure, but its predictability is like letting the air out of a balloon: the tension of the anticipation evaporates with the arrival of the commonplace idea expressed in the objective complement.

How about a more interesting possibility:

> Jack considers jogging <u>a necessary evil</u>.

That is a little more unexpected but still falls within a reader's range of anticipated responses.

So, let's move beyond that range:

> Jack considers jogging <u>a waste of time</u>.

This one would probably surprise most readers. Now, let's push a little further:

> Jack considers jogging <u>beneficial only to manufacturers of running shoes</u>.

This version returns to the first objective complement, but then undercuts it with the following phrases.

The second sentence clearly needs more information to say anything useful:

> Jill thinks it.

Here, the subject, verb, object pattern, though grammatically complete, says nothing useful. Even if we put it in context with the previous sentence so that the pronoun *it* refers to *jogging*, readers still will be left wondering what Jill thinks about jogging. That sets up another situation where the reader will try to guess what will come next. Jack considers jogging beneficial, but what does his partner in walking up the hill think? Does she agree? Because they seem to be a pair, readers might naturally assume they will think alike. In adding a sentence to the one about Jack, the writer has two choices. One is to start as the sentence is written above. The other is to provide a **transitional phrase** that will alert readers to what is coming up. Although this is the first time we discuss transitional phrases as a matter of style, their use is not particular to objective complement templates. They should also be contemplated in all of the templates.

Let's say, you, as writer, decide that Jill disagrees with Jack and therefore phrase your sentence according to the first choice:

> Jill thinks it a waste of time.

Alternatively, you might decide to prepare your reader by inserting a transitional phrase at the beginning of the sentence:

> On the other hand, Jill thinks it a waste of time.

This is a stylistic choice. If your interest is absolute clarity, as is often encouraged in college writing classes, you would pick the option including the transitional phrase. If, on the other hand, you would rather surprise your reader, you would pick the version without such a phrase. This choice can be seen most clearly when the two versions of the two sentences are presented together:

> Jack considers jogging beneficial. Jill thinks it a waste of time.

> Jack considers jogging beneficial. On the other hand, Jill thinks it a waste of time.

Finally, notice that in the second version, there is another stylistic choice involving the placement of the transitional phrase. That phrase is adverbial, and as such, can be placed, as you have seen before, in various optional slots. We have it at the beginning of the sentence, but it can also appear after the subject. (Other positions are technically possible but unlikely.) Placing it after the subject delays, however briefly, alerting the reader to the change in direction:

> Jill, on the other hand, thinks it a waste of time.

The difference is slight but noticeable. Beginning with *Jill* prompts the reader to remember her relationship with Jack and thus to think she might well agree with him. Beginning with the transitional phrase immediately alerts the reader to a change of direction. Thus, when Jill follows the phrase, the reader is prepared for finding out that she has a different opinion.

Such small differences can add up over the course of a piece of writing and represent the kind of sentence-level fine tuning that leads to clearer, more effective writing.

Matters of Usage

Again, we are dealing with the usual suspects: subject/verb agreement and pronoun case.

Subject-Verb Agreement

Now that we have gone over this problem several times, let's focus more specifically on one phrasing that causes problems. Examine the two sentences below:

> Jack and Jill think climbing hills for a pail of water a burden.
> Jack, along with Jill, thinks climbing hills for a pail of water a burden.

Clearly, these two sentences seem to be saying exactly the same thing, but there is one grammatical difference. In the first, the verb *think* is plural, while in the second the verb *thinks* is singular.

A close look at the phrasing reveals the reason for this difference. The first sentence has a compound subject, meaning two nouns connected by the conjunction *and*. A compound subject is considered to be plural, and thus the verb chosen is that which agrees with a plural subject. In the second sentence, Jill is not part of the subject. In our terms, she is not in the subject slot. Rather, she appears in an optional slot as the object of a prepositional phrase. Thus, she cannot grammatically hold hands with Jack, who remains the singular subject.

In a similar way, when the subject is followed by optional slots that delay the entrance of the verb into the template, and if the last of those optional slots is a prepositional phrase with an object of a different number than the subject, an agreement issue might pop up:

> Jack, an aspiring scholar sitting in the library surrounded by notes
> on index cards, considers books his friends.

Because of the distance between the subject *Jack* and the verb *considers*, and because the noun immediately before the verb is the plural *books* as the object of the preposition, it is possible that that noun might be thought of as the subject, thus producing the agreement error of *consider*.

Pronoun Case

In this template, as in others involving objects, the issue of hypercorrectness is likely to occur in sentences such as this one:

> Jill considers Jack and I good buddies.

Here the temptation to seem to be so very correct leads to using the subjective form of the first person pronoun as the second object of the verb *considers* in an objective complement structure. The proper noun *Jack* seems to answer the need for an objective form after the verb and shields the reader's ear from hearing how wrong *I* would sound if it came first:

> Jill considers I and Jack good buddies.

In this arrangement, it is much more likely that your ear will tell you that the pronoun should be in the objective case:

> Jill considers me and Jack good buddies.

To make the point even more emphatic, consider eliminating Jack from the situation altogether:

> Jill considers me a good buddy.

Possible Ambiguity

Thus far, the verbs in our examples have been *think* and *consider*, and they are probably the most common verb choices in this template. However, there is another common verb that sometimes appears in this template, one that can also lead to grammatically ambiguous situations.

Look at the following two sentences:

> Jill made Jack a delicious cake.
> Jill made Jack her best friend.

These two look almost identical. The grammatical constituents in each are the same, and they appear in their templates in the same order:

> Noun   Verb   Noun   Noun

The proper nouns *Jill* and *Jack* are the same; the verb is the same; and a noun modified by an adjective in the noun phrase follows the verb in each.

And yet they clearly are different. The first is a direct/indirect object template, while the second is a direct object/objective complement template. A simple test reveals the difference.

The first can be changed into the alternative syntax of its template:

> Jill made a delicious cake for Jack.

Here the second noun turns out to be the direct object, while the first can now be seen as the indirect object, showing up as the object of the preposition *for* in this alternate version of the direct/indirect object template.

Now, see what happens if that test is applied to the second sentence:

> Jill made her best friend for Jack.

The noun phrase *her best friend* cannot serve as the direct object as *a delicious cake* does in the other sentence. That is because *her best friend* is an objective complement.

For further proof that the second sentence is an objective complement template, we can apply the linking verb test to the second sentence:

> Jack is her best friend.

This does not work in the first sentence, since it would yield the following ridiculous idea:

> Jack is a delicious cake.

That should seal the deal.

What we have here, then, is a case of grammatical ambiguity, similar to the one involving the past participle in the passive voice version of the transitive verb template (pp. 67–68). Readers coming across a sentence beginning with a noun, followed by a form of *make*, and then followed by another noun will not be sure what template is being presented:

> Jill made Jack...

Reading that beginning offers three possibilities. The first is that *Jack* is the direct object of *made* and that there will be no other noun, or noun equivalent, following. This is grammatically possible, but unlikely. Perhaps in a police drama, where *made* carries the context-dependent meaning of revealing somebody's actual identity, you could encounter a sentence such as this:

> Jill made Jack as an undercover cop.

Otherwise, however, readers will expect another noun to follow *Jack*, and after reading or hearing it they will have to determine which template they are dealing with. In most cases, context will make it clear.

Exercises

I. Sentences with Objective Complements

A. Using one of the verb choices, and choosing among the possibilities in the other slots, compose ten sentences in this pattern:

Subject	Verb	Direct Object	Objective Complement	
Noun Pronoun Gerund Infinitive	think consider make	Noun Pronoun Gerund	(to be)	Noun Adjective

1. _____

2. _____

3. _____

4. _____

5. _____

6. _____

7. _____

8. _____

9. _____

10. _____

B. Create direct object/objective complement template sentences according to the patterns indicated, using this key for abbreviations:

N	Noun
P	Pronoun
G	Gerund
I	Infinitive
V	Verb
PP	Prepositional Phrase
ADJ	Adjective
ADV	Adverb

1. N   V   N   N

_____

2. N   V   P   ADJ

_____

3. PP   PP   P   V   P   ADJ   N

_____

4. N   PP   ADV   V   N   N

_____

5. G   N   V   N   ADJ

_____

II. Choosing the Correct Template

Indicate whether the sentences below are direct/indirect object templates or objective complement templates. Explain your answer.

1. The local newspaper made the new regulation known.
2. Jill made Jack a New Year's promise.
3. Jack made Jill a promise.
4. Jill bought Jack a new bucket.
5. Jack and Jill considered indoor plumbing a good investment.

III. Usage Matters

The sentences below have either subject/verb or pronoun case usage issues. Pick the preferred choice in the parentheses for each sentence.

1. Jack considers Jill and (he, him) a good match.
2. Jill, as opposed to her friends and family, (believe, believes) buying a demo model a good deal.
3. Jill's neighbor Humpty Dumpty, along with Jack, (consider, considers) her beautiful.
4. Everyone in the group of philatelists (think, thinks) the new stamp a mistake.
5. Jill's mother considers (she, her) and Jill best friends.

CHAPTER SEVEN

Compound Templates

The previous chapters presented the five basic templates out of which English sentences can be created. Every formally constructed English sentence contains at least one subject/verb combination organized into one of these templates. Such a combination is also called a **clause**. Although thus far all of our illustrations have been of sentences containing one clause, a sentence can, and often does, include more than one clause. It is now time to move on to the much more common syntactic patterns of multi-clause sentences.

To begin, we have to distinguish between **independent** and **dependent** clauses. (Alternative terminology substitutes **main** for "independent" and **subordinate** for "dependent.") An independent clause is one that, in more formal writing, can and should be punctuated as a sentence by itself, while a dependent clause, again in more formal writing, can and should be connected to an independent clause partner. Punctuating a dependent clause by itself as a sentence is considered a **fragment** and generally should not be done in formal writing, such as that required in college courses.

Compound Sentences and Coordination

The simplest way to move from a one-clause sentence, such as those we have been working with, to a two-clause sentence is to combine two independent clauses into one sentence. Such a sentence is called a **compound sentence**. (As the subsequent chapters will indicate, you can compose a **complex sentence** by hooking a dependent clause to an independent clause.)

To create a compound sentence, simply present them one after the other and then insert a connector between them. That connector can be a semicolon, or it can be one of a small list of combining words called **coordinating conjunctions**, which are usually preceded by a comma. While all conjunctions work to link constituents together, coordinating conjunctions are so called because they connect constituents of equal grammatical status. In the case now being discussed, the two equal constituents are independent clauses.

An independent clause is one that can be punctuated as a sentence, beginning with a capital letter and ending with a period. All of the sentences you have seen in the previous chapters have been independent clauses. Another independent clause can be added by starting another sentence:

> Jack and Jill went up the hill. They wanted to fill their pail with water.

Writing aimed at beginning readers usually strings together these kinds of sentences because they are easier to process than the more complicated ones this chapter introduces. Writing aimed at more experienced readers would probably combine these two sentences in one of the ways suggested below:

Semicolon: Jack and Jill went up the hill; they wanted to fill their pail with water.
Conjunction: Jack and Jill went up the hill, for they wanted to fill their pail with water.

The first option, adding the semicolon between the two clauses, represents a very modest change from simply having a period after the first clause and a capital letter beginning the next one. The second option, adding a conjunction, adds meaning because the conjunction itself indicates a relationship between the second clause and the first. In this case, the conjunction *for* tells the reader that there is a cause/effect relationship between the two clauses. Specifically, the second clause is the cause and the first clause is the effect. Stated another way, what the conjunction tells the reader is that Jack and Jill went up the hill (effect) because they wanted to fill their pail with water (cause).

English has only a small number of coordinating conjunctions, and each one provides the reader with a different understanding of the relationship between the two clauses. Table 7.1 presents the coordinating conjunctions and their meanings.

TABLE 7.1: COORDINATING CONJUNCTIONS

Coordinating conjunction	Meaning	Example
and	tells the reader that the second clause provides additional content, similar to what is in the first clause	Jack and Jill went up the hill, and then they rested.
but	tells the reader to be aware of a shift in direction, or a contradiction of what the first clause states	Jack went up the hill, but Jill stayed home.

or	tells the reader that a choice is possible	Jill would get water, or she would settle for juice.
nor	adds another negative example	Jack did not like pickles, nor would he eat cucumbers.
for	tells the reader that the second clause is the cause of the point made in the first clause	Jill stayed home, for she was sick that day.
so	tells the reader that the second clause results from the first	Jack was sick of carrying water, so he stayed home.
yet	tells the reader that the second clause qualifies what the first clause says	Jack walked up the hill, yet his progress was slow.

An effect similar to adding a coordinating conjunction can be created by insert-ing a semi-colon followed by a transitional word called a **conjunctive adverb**. As that term suggests, the form is part conjunction, like the coordinating conjunctions above, but also part adverb, meaning it serves a modifying function. Here is how that alternative could be used in place of *yet*:

Jack walked up the hill; <u>however</u>, his progress was slow.

As you can see, these two sentences say almost exactly the same thing, namely that Jack walked slowly up the hill. Although there is quite a long list of conjunctive adverbs, the most common include *moreover, therefore, nonetheless,* and *furthermore.*

Having seen how two independent clauses can be combined to form a compound sentence, let's take a look at what is being combined. As you have seen, independent clauses can occur in the different templates covered in previous chapters. Sometimes in a compound sentence, both clauses will be in the same template:

Jack walked slowly up the hill, and Jill trudged up behind him.

In this sentence, both independent clauses are intransitive verb templates.

We can construct a compound sentence with two linking verb templates:

Jack is overweight, yet he appears fit.

Or two transitive verb templates:

Jack liked the job, but Jill hated it.

Or two direct/indirect object templates:

> Jack bought Jill a kitten, but she gave it to her cousin.

Or two object/objective complement templates:

> Jack thought the kitten adorable, but Jill found it annoying.

However, in constructing compound sentences, it is not necessary for each clause to use the same template. One example will suffice:

> Jill carried the pail of water, for Jack was hung over.

Here the first clause is a transitive template while the second is a linking verb template.

Finally, as you will see later on, although we have been concentrating here on two-clause sentences, there is theoretically no limit to the number of clauses any one sentence can contain.

The Basic Templates

Up to now, the constituents for each template have been indicated in the drop-down menus showing the choices that English syntax provides. Now, as we deal with longer, more complicated sentences, the templates available for each clause in compound and complex sentences will be specified. The choices for compound sentences at the clause level can be illustrated this way:

| Intransitive Template
Linking Template
Transitive Template
Direct/Indirect Object Template
Object/Objective Complement Template | ;

, and
, but
, for
, so
, yet
, or
, nor

; however,
; therefore,
; moreover, | Intransitive Template
Linking Template
Transitive Template
Direct/Indirect Object Template
Object/Objective Complement Template |

You can see that only a suggestive list of three conjunctive adverbs is included.

Matters of Style

Your first stylistic choice in composing a compound sentence is to decide among the three possibilities for joining the two clauses: a semicolon alone, a comma and a coordinating conjunction, or a semicolon and a conjunctive adverb. Each choice produces a different effect, as demonstrated in these variations applied to one of the example sentences above:

> Jack ran up the hill; Jill trudged up behind him.
> Jack ran up the hill, but Jill trudged up behind him.
> Jack ran up the hill; however, Jill trudged up behind him.

In the first version, only the semicolon alerts the reader to the upcoming second independent clause. The result is a kind of bare-bones impression that leaves the reader the job of figuring out the relationship between the two clauses. Depending upon context and on what the second clause says, that relationship can take any number of different forms. As expressed above, it would seem that the two clauses of the sentence taken together offer a simple statement of fact. But the verb in the second—*trudged*—suggests a little more meaning. To trudge is to walk with difficulty or reluctance, which provides some contrast with the more positive *ran* of the first clause. Additionally, the fact that Jill *trudged* behind Jack also contributes a nuance of meaning. It suggests, perhaps, an unhappiness with their joint water-seeking venture.

The point is that joining these two clauses with only a semicolon requires the reader to work to squeeze out the meaning. Many how-to writing books say that the writer's job is to make life easy for the reader, and that is certainly true when the goal of the writing is clarity, as it is in much expository writing. However, there are situations in which the approach illustrated in this version can be desirable. In these circumstances, the writer might choose to sacrifice a little clarity for tension, which in this context means creating a desire in the reader for that same clarity. That desire, in turn, motivates the reader to concentrate and to look for the missing certainty.

The other choices in combining these two clauses emphasize clarity. In the second possibility, the clauses are joined by a comma followed by a coordinating conjunction:

> Jack ran up the hill, <u>but</u> Jill trudged up behind him.

Here the coordinating conjunction alerts the reader to a change in direction that will be expressed in the second clause. A somewhat different effect can be created by employing *and* as the conjunction:

> Jack ran up the hill, <u>and</u> Jill trudged up behind him.

In this case, the conjunction only indicates that the following clause will most likely provide similar information. Jack might have run, and Jill might have trudged, but there is not the clear sense of a negative attitude found in the *but* version. In fact, written this way, the sentence might suggest that Jill would have moved faster if she were able, that she was trying, unsuccessfully, to keep up with Jack.

Switching to the third possible combining technique involves using the semi-colon followed by a conjunctive adverb:

> Jack ran up the hill; <u>however</u>, Jill trudged up behind him.
> Jack ran up the hill; <u>moreover</u>, Jill trudged up behind him.

You can see that the two conjunctive adverbs perform a function similar to the two coordinating conjunctions. The conjunction *but* is replaced by *however*, and the conjunction *and* is replaced by *moreover*. Otherwise these sentences are very similar to the ones using conjunctions. The change in punctuation, however, does provide a subtle difference. Semicolons are stronger than commas, so they produce a sharper interruption in the flow of language. Moreover, they seem more appropriate in fairly formal writing, while commas can fit comfortably into either casual or formal contexts.

Another stylistic choice in constructing a compound sentence is to decide whether or not you want to work with the same template for each clause. The advantage of employing the same template for each clause is that you will be working in the same (parallel) structure, which provides an excellent opportunity to create emphasis through either repetition or contrast. See how this works in the translation of a famous sentence by the Roman emperor Julius Caesar:

> I came, I saw, I conquered.

Here we have a series of three two-word intransitive verb templates. The subject of each template is the same, the pronoun *I*. But the verb changes, moving through the progression of arriving, surveying, and winning the battle.

Centuries after Caesar, King Jan III of Poland offered a variation of this famous statement, which can be translated this way:

> We came, we saw, God conquered.

Apparently King Jan's ego was not quite as elevated as was Caesar's, as the king gives credit to God for his success while Caesar takes the credit for himself. Jan's version builds on the reader's familiarity with the original, and then changes the subject in the third clause, creating a very effective and surprising contrast.

Let's wrap up this point with two more examples, the first from a fourteenth-century work of devotion:

> Man proposes, but God disposes.

Here both the subject and the verb change in the second clause, while the conjunction *but* sets the reader up to receive the contrasting statement. In addition, the rhyme of the two verbs increases the effect of the structural repetition.

The second is far more recent, one of the many quotable lines written by Martin Luther King, Jr.:

> Science investigates; religion interprets.

Here, in two intransitive templates, King offers a resolution to the perceived conflict between science and religion, with the nouns for those sources of knowledge occupying the subject slots of the templates. The verbs both express a positive action rather than conflicting values, and the fact that each verb begins with the same *in* syllable adds emphasis. King gets quite a lot of stylistic punch in four words addressing one of our fundamental issues.

These examples are suggestive of the wide range of stylistic possibilities available in this template. There are many other possibilities involving clauses composed in the other templates, or sentences in which different templates are employed for each of the independent clauses. The exercises for this chapter provide some opportunity to explore these other options.

Matters of Usage

By far the most common usage problem in this template involves punctuation, specifically **comma splices** occurring between the two independent clauses.

A comma splice can be defined as the use of a comma where a stronger mark of punctuation is strongly preferred. Those stronger marks of punctuation include a period, a semicolon, and, less often, a colon or a dash. The first of these provides the strongest guideline in identifying the problem area: if a period can properly replace the comma, you are dealing with a comma splice; the two are not interchangeable. The period test works because by definition an independent clause is one that can be punctuated as a sentence, starting with a capital letter and concluding with a period. The word *splice* means to tie two things together, and in the phrase *comma splice*, what is being tied together are two independent clauses. In formal usage, a comma, the weakest mark of punctuation, is not seen as strong enough for this job, which calls for one of the comma's stronger, more emphatic relatives.

If you look back to the possible ways to join two independent clauses in this template (pp. 102–03), you will see that these choices include a semicolon alone, a semicolon plus a conjunctive adverb, and a coordinating conjunction preceded by a comma. The most common usage error among these choices is using a comma in either of the places where a semi-colon is preferred:

With the semicolon:	Jack walked up the hill; Jill trudged up behind him.
With a comma:	Jack walked up the hill, Jill trudged up behind him.
With a semicolon:	Jack walked up the hill; moreover, Jill trudged up behind him.
With a comma:	Jack walked up the hill, moreover, Jill trudged up behind him.

In each pair, the one employing the comma would be considered a comma splice. And between these two problem areas, by far the most difficult to eradicate is the one involving the conjunctive adverb. Writers, with good reason, feel that the conjunctive adverb does the same job as the coordinating conjunction, which requires only a comma for formal correctness. However, as reasonable as that supposition appears to be, it ignores the fact that the conjunctive adverb is, as its name indicates, an adverb. And because adverbs can modify in either direction—either what comes before them or what follows them—it is necessary to use punctuation to tell the reader in which direction the modification is intended. Read the example sentence above and stop after the conjunctive adverb:

Jack walked up the hill, moreover,

At this point, it is not clear whether *moreover* modifies what has already preceded it, or what might follow it. In the first instance, the word would indicate that the fact that Jack walked up the hill is in addition to some other action he had taken, perhaps finding his bucket. In the second instance, the word would suggest either that he would then do something else or, as is the case in this sentence, that somebody else, namely Jill, is doing a similar action.

The ambidextrous nature of the conjunctive adverb can be illustrated this way:

← ,moreover, →

Placing commas around the word does not tell the reader which directional modification is intended because the modification jumps over the weak comma. However, the modification cannot jump over the semicolon, so one possible direction is eliminated. In most cases, it is the backward direction that needs to be blocked, as the conjunctive adverb most usually modifies the upcoming clause.

Jack walked up the hill; moreover, → Jill trudged up behind him.

This particular comma splice issue is very common, even in writing that is otherwise fairly consistent with formal usage. Nonetheless, as this example illustrates, comma splices create a moment's confusion for the reader. Since avoiding such reader confusion is generally a good idea, a careful writer will use a semicolon with conjunctive adverbs to combine two independent clauses.

Finally, it is useful to note that because conjunctive adverbs, as adverbs, can be bracketed with commas and moved around in single-clause templates, student writers can reasonably form the impression that commas alone are sufficient punctuation:

> Jack, therefore, felt too tired to fetch the water.
> Jack felt, therefore, too tired to fetch the water.

And commonly, these conjunctive adverbs start independent clause templates:

> Therefore, Jack felt too tired to fetch the water.

In each of these cases, the adverb's modifying function, i.e., indicating that the clause expresses the effect of some condition or action, is clear. Perhaps a little less clear is the combining function, because in these sentences, *therefore* combines its independent clause with something already expressed.

This common practice of placing conjunctive adverbs between commas in various positions in single independent clause templates needs to be understood as an entirely different situation from the preferred punctuation of these combining words between independent clauses in the same sentence.

Exercises

I. Compound Sentences

A. Using one of the template choices for each independent clause, and choosing among the combining possibilities, compose ten sentences in this pattern:

| Intransitive Template
Linking Template
Transitive Template
Direct/Indirect Object Template
Object/Objective Complement Template | ;

, and
, but
, for
, so
, yet
, or
, nor

; however,
; therefore,
; moreover, | Intransitive Template
Linking Template
Transitive Template
Direct/Indirect Object Template
Object/Objective Complement Template |

1. _____

2. _____

3. _____

4. _____

5. _____

6. _____

7. _____

8. _____

9. _____

10. _____

B. Create compound template sentences according to the patterns indicated, using this key for abbreviations:

N   Noun
P   Pronoun

G	Gerund
I	Infinitive
V	Verb
PP	Prepositional Phrase
ADJ	Adjective
ADV	Adverb
DO	Direct Object
IO	Indirect Object
CC	Coordinating Conjunction
CA	Conjunctive Adverb

After each sentence, indicate what form template has been created for each independent clause. Be sure to use preferred punctuation.

1. N   V   ADJ   CC   N   V   ADJ

_____

Types of Clause Templates:_____

2. PP   N   V   N   CA   PP   P   V   N

_____

Types of Clause Templates:_____

3. N   V   N   N   CC   P   ADV   V   P

_____

Types of Clause Templates:_____

4. N   V   PP   CC   P   V   PP

_____

Types of Clause Templates:_____

5. N   ADV   V   N   CA   N   V   ADV   ADJ

_____

Types of Clause Templates:_____

C. Construct your own sentences with the following combination of clause templates. Choose how you want to combine the clauses, using either coordinating conjunctions or conjunctive adverbs. Be careful of the punctuation used with these combining methods.

1. Linking Verb   Linking Verb

_____

2. Intransitive Verb   Transitive Verb

_____

3. Direct/Indirect Object   Linking Verb

_____

4. Transitive Verb   Objective Complement

_____

5. Intransitive Verb   Linking Verb

_____

II. Comma Splices

A. Check the punctuation in the following and indicate if it is correct (C) or incorrect. If incorrect, indicate the preferred punctuation.

1. Jack climbed up the hill, however, Jill stayed home._____
2. Jill enjoys a cup of tea, but Jack prefers coffee._____
3. Jack is sorry about the bucket fiasco; moreover, he feels responsible. _____
4. Jill walked the dog and Jack fed the cat._____
5. Jack and Jill walked up the hill, so they could get water._____

B. Now rewrite the sentences above using either a semicolon alone or a coordinating conjunction preceded by a comma. Offer an explanation of the different effect produced by each version.

1. _____

Effect:_____

2._____

Effect:_____

3._____

Effect:_____

4. _____

Effect:_____

5. _____

Effect:_____

CHAPTER EIGHT

Dependent Clause Templates I: Adverb Clauses

The final three chapters will describe three types of dependent clause: adverb clauses, adjective clauses, and noun clauses. In preferred usage, none of these can stand alone as a sentence, because a dependent clause punctuated as a sentence is regarded as a **fragment**. And because fragments are discouraged in preferred usage situations, a dependent clause should normally be connected to an independent clause to form an acceptable sentence. Only in the hands of a skillful writer in carefully defined circumstances should this general usage rule be ignored. Examples will be offered in the Matters of Style section.

Adverb Clauses

As the name suggests, these dependent clauses function as adverbs. In contrast to adjectives, which modify only nouns or other adjectives (as you will see in the next chapter), adverbs modify a variety of other constituents, such as verbs, adjectives, verbals, adverbs, and even whole clauses. In the following examples, the first shows a simple adverb and the second an adverb clause:

> Jack whistled <u>happily</u>.
> Jack whistled <u>because he was happy</u>.

> Jill's pace was <u>too</u> fast.
> Jill's pace was faster <u>after she fell</u>.

<u>Carelessly</u> carrying the bucket, Jack spilled the water.
<u>When he lost his grip carrying the bucket</u>, Jack spilled the water.

Jack works <u>very</u> hard.
Jack works harder <u>when he is hungry</u>.

<u>Reluctantly</u>, they walked up the hill.
<u>Although they were tired</u>, they walked up the hill.

Notice that all of these adverb clauses would sound and feel incomplete if punctuated as a sentence:

Because he was happy.
After she fell.
When he lost his grip carrying the bucket.
When he is hungry.
Although they were tired.

Now see what happens when the introductory word is removed:

He was happy.
She fell.
He lost his grip carrying the bucket.
He is hungry.
They were tired.

All of these now sound and feel like sentences, although not very interesting ones because they don't say very much. Grammarians call the introductory words—i.e., the ones we just removed—**subordinating conjunctions** because they make the clauses they introduce subordinate to, or dependent on, an independent clause. All clauses contain a subject/verb combination in one of the available templates. That is true for adverb clauses as well, but the subordinating conjunctions introducing them make them incomplete unless they are attached to an independent clause.

Traditional grammar divides the kind of modification performed by adverbs into such categories as time, concession, cause, and so forth:

Time: <u>When he lost his grip carrying the bucket</u>, Jack spilled the water.
Cause: Jack whistled <u>because he was happy</u>.
Concession: <u>Although they were tired</u>, they walked up the hill.

These are notional definitions (see p. 14) because the classification depends upon the meaning being communicated. There is nothing wrong with such definitions, but they do not add much to our understanding of the structure of the sentence and sometimes can be difficult to apply. In the first sentence above, although the adverb clause clearly indicates time, the moment Jack lost his grip, it also suggests causation, in that he spilled the water because he lost his grip. Compounding this difficulty is the fact that some subordinating conjunctions themselves are ambiguous: for example, *since* can indicate either a condition or a time:

Condition: <u>Since</u> Jill was tired, she stayed home.
Time: Jack and Jill had carried that bucket <u>since</u> they were young.

One of the further distinguishing features of adverb clauses is that they are much more movable than adjectives and adjective clauses. In all of the examples above, the adverb clause can almost always either precede or follow the independent clause to which it is attached, as in this one example:

Jack whistled <u>because he was happy</u>.

or

<u>Because he was happy</u>, Jack whistled.

Choosing whether or not to begin with the adverb clause raises both stylistic and usage issues to be discussed later in this chapter.

The Basic Templates

Again, as you saw in the previous chapter, these more complicated sentence structures can, and often do, involve combinations of the various templates. Here, then, is an illustration of these possibilities using a list of the more common subordinating conjunctions. In addition, as noted above, the adverb clause can either precede or follow the independent clause.

<u>Independent Clause</u>	<u>Conjunction</u>	<u>Adverb Clause</u>
Intransitive Template	because	Intransitive Template
Linking Template	when	Linking Template
Transitive Template	so that	Transitive Template
Direct/Indirect Object Template	if	Direct/Indirect Object Template
Object/Objective Complement Template	as	Object/Objective Complement Template
	since	
	provided that	

Conjunction	Adverb Clause	Independent Clause
Because When So that If As Since Provided that	Intransitive Template Linking Template Transitive Template Direct/Indirect Object Template Object/Objective Complement Template	Intransitive Template Linking Template Transitive Template Direct/Indirect Object Template Object/Objective Complement Template

Clearly, there are too many combinations of templates to illustrate, but a few examples will suffice:

Because Jack was sick, Jill carried the bucket by herself.

Here the adverb clause beginning the sentence is a linking verb template, while the independent clause is a transitive verb template. The adverb clause is introduced by the conjunction *because*.

Jill called Jack lazy when he slept in bed all day.

This one begins with an independent clause in an objective complement template, followed by the adverb clause, introduced by the conjunction *when*, in an intransitive template.

Jack promised an improvement in his work habits provided that his pay increases.

This example begins with an independent clause in a transitive template, followed by an adverb clause, introduced by the conjunction *provided that*, in an intransitive template.

Jill was happy since Jack told her his idea.

This final example begins with an independent clause in a linking template, followed by an adverb clause, introduced by the conjunction *since*, in a direct/indirect object template.

There are, of course, many other conjunctions that can introduce an adverb clause and other combinations of clauses. You will get an opportunity to explore some of these possibilities in the exercises.

Matters of Style

The chief issue is the question of whether or not to begin a sentence with the adverb clause. Adverb clauses must be attached to an independent clause, but the order of the clauses is not prescribed. So why is there a problem?

The answer is the conjunction that introduces adverb clauses. Perhaps some of you have been told by a teacher that you should not begin a sentence with a word like *because*. You might even have read such a prohibition in a textbook. But as you have seen above, there appears to be nothing wrong with doing just that. The "rule" seems to run counter to the acceptable structures provided by English syntax.

And it does. (This previous sentence would also seem to violate the same rule, but notice that I used it for a particular stylistic effect.) In both cases student writers are told that certain words such as *and* or *because*, along with a number of others, should not begin sentences. The reason for this prohibition is simply to prevent fragments. Because subordinating conjunctions make the clauses they introduce dependent clauses, if the sentence stops with a period at the end of that dependent clause, the result is a fragment. Careful readers will no doubt observe that the previous sentence begins with one of the prohibited words—*because*—but its clause does not stop with a period. If it did, it would be this fragment:

Because subordinating conjunctions make the clauses they introduce dependent clauses.

Those same careful readers might also have noticed that in that same sentence one adverb clause is followed by another one, this one introduced by the conjunction *if*, before we get to the short independent clause:

The result is a fragment.

This one sentence underscores an important stylistic point. First, it is the nature of a dependent clause to create anticipation in readers who recognize that an independent clause should follow. This recognition provides the anticipation. The adverb clause by itself is unsatisfactory; it leaves readers hanging. The independent clause must follow to resolve the tension of that anticipation. In the sentence under consideration, the independent clause is short and to the point, and therefore satisfying. It's like that first sip of cold water on a hot day.

Second, this sentence illustrates another important stylistic point: there is no limit to the number of dependent clauses that can precede (or follow) an independent clause. This sentence has two, but other sentences can have many more:

Because it was hot, because he was working hard, and because he was starting to feel faint, Jack asked Jill for a glass of cold water.

This sentence begins with three adverb clauses. In the exercises at the end of the chapter, you will have a chance to check out a famous sentence from a literary classic that begins with many more than three adverb clauses (see pp. 126-27).

Beginning a sentence with a dependent clause, or clauses, can usefully create a tension that will be resolved by the concluding independent clause. This tension can be observed even in sentences employing an adverbial prepositional phrase rather than a dependent clause:

> In the beginning, God created the heaven and the earth.

That very familiar first sentence of the King James Bible starts with just such a prepositional phrase, followed by the independent clause. If that phrase were placed after the clause, the resulting sentence would offer the same information, but without the tension:

> God created the heaven and the earth in the beginning.

Stylistically, this version lacks tension. Since readers already know the main and very important fact that God created the heavens and the earth, the inclusion of when that happened reads more like a footnote. But placed at the beginning of the sentence, the phrase acts as a teaser to whet the readers' appetite. Something happened in the beginning. What was it? The independent clause that follows provides the resounding answer.

In a similar manner, see the difference when an adverb clause instead of a prepositional phrase either follows or precedes the independent clause:

> Jack spilled the water because he tripped.

> or

> Because he tripped, Jack spilled the water.

When the independent clause comes first, there is no tension because the reader already knows the important point, that being that Jack spilled the water. Beginning with the adverb clause does create, even in this very simple sentence, a certain degree of tension waiting to be resolved by the independent clause. Readers learn that Jack tripped, but they do not know why they are being told this fact. The independent clause answers that question by indicating the result of the trip, namely that Jack spilled the water.

In certain situations, when the independent clause expresses a fact familiar to the reader, placing it first can create anticipation to be resolved in the following adverb clause:

> Jack fell down because...

Here the reader who is familiar with this part of the rhyme might anticipate discovering causation:

> Jack fell down because he stepped into a hole in the ground.
> Jack fell down because Jill pushed him from behind.
> Jack fell down because a rabbit startled him.

In all these instances, the adverb clause answers the unanswered question in the original rhyme.

The stylistic point here is the value of emphasis. As a writer, you decide whether or not you want to emphasize a certain point. If you do, withholding the independent clause to the end of the sentence is a good way to produce that emphasis. It is important to note, however, that you do not want to overuse this device. Doing so will significantly lessen its effectiveness in creating emphasis. Any stylistic choice should be employed selectively, as will be seen in the following section. Furthermore, in many writing situations, providing immediate clarity is more important than building tension. In such situations, it might well be preferable to begin with the main point you want to communicate to your readers and leave the details to modifiers appearing later in the sentence.

Matters of Usage

Here style and usage intersect. One of the usage problems associated with any dependent clause, but particularly with adverb clauses, is the possibility of writing a fragment by punctuating the clause as a sentence without connecting it to the necessary independent clause. Writing handbooks usually warn against doing that, and, as noted above, to prevent those problems, such texts often proscribe beginning sentences with the subordinating conjunctions that lead into adverb clauses.

Fragments are frowned upon in most formal writing situations because they confuse and often irritate readers. They have the effect of jamming on the brakes in a car for no apparent reason. You read the dependent clause at the beginning of the sentence and fully expect the sentence to continue into an independent clause, but first you run into a period and then the capital letter announcing the beginning of an entirely different sentence.

For these reasons, fragments are *generally* to be avoided. The key word here is "generally." Because fragments startle readers in the same way that jamming down the brakes does, they can be an effective stylistic device if offered deliberately by writers who know very well what they are doing:

> Everyday Jack and Jill woke up to their morning chore. Once again they would have to take their wooden bucket down from its hook next to the door. They would perhaps eat their breakfast and wash their dishes in water left over from their last trip up the hill. Then in rain or shine, hot or cold, they each would take a handle of the bucket and head up the hill. Although today would be different.

This paragraph ends with an adverb clause standing by itself, and thus it is a fragment. And because it is a fragment after a series of ordinary, grammatically whole sentences, it calls attention to itself, and in calling attention to itself it provides emphasis. In this case, that emphasis is useful because it suddenly changes the direction established by the previous flow of language, which describes the humdrum, daily routine of Jack and Jill. The reader is lulled into the very ordinariness of each day for the couple only to be startled, in a good way, by the fragment that announces that today will be different. Some writers would further increase the emphasis of the fragment by making it a new, one-line paragraph:

> Everyday Jack and Jill woke up to their morning chore. Once again they would have to take their wooden bucket down from its hook next to the door. They would perhaps eat their breakfast and wash their dishes in water left over from their last trip up the hill. Then in rain or shine, hot or cold, they each would take a handle of the bucket and head up the hill.
>
> Although today would be different.

These two changes, a conscious fragment and its placement as a one-line paragraph, create maximum emphasis. But such a stylistic extravagance should only be used very occasionally, since repetition will rapidly diminish its effectiveness.

One other usage issue particular to adverb clauses, although a rather minor one, is the question of preferred punctuation. When the adverb clause precedes the independent clause, preferred usage suggests placing a comma after the adverb clause:

> Because he tripped, Jack spilled the water.

Conversely, if the adverb clause follows the independent clause, the comma is usually omitted:

> Jack spilled the water because he tripped.

Perhaps the reasoning for this preference is that anything that delays the entrance of the subject in the sentence is generally followed by a comma:

One word:	Carelessly, Jack spilled the water.
Phrase:	For the second time, Jack spilled the water.
Clause:	Because he tripped, Jack spilled the water.

Whatever the reason, this comma placement is preferred usage. Ignoring this preference by eliminating the comma speeds up the flow of language at that point and might serve a stylistic purpose.

Exercises

I. Sentences with Adverb Clauses

A. Using one of the template choices for each clause, and choosing among the conjunctions listed, or providing one of your own, compose ten sentences. Indicate which template has been employed for each clause.

Independent Clause	**Conjunction**	**Adverb Clause**
Intransitive Template Linking Template Transitive Template Direct/Indirect Object Template Object/Objective Complement Template	because when so that if as since provided that	Intransitive Template Linking Template Transitive Template Direct/Indirect Object Template Object/Objective Complement Template

1. _____

Clause Template:_____

2. _____

Clause Template:_____

3. _____

Clause Template:_____

4. _____

Clause Template:_____

5. _____

Clause Template:_____

6. _____

Clause Template:_____

7. _____

Clause Template:_____

8. _____

Clause Template:_____

9. _____

Clause Template:_____

10. _____

Clause Template:_____

B. Now pick five of your sentences and reverse the order of the clauses by beginning with the adverb clause. Consider the different effect created by the reversed order.

Conjunction	**Adverb Clause**	**Independent Clause**
Because When So that If As Since Provided that	Intransitive Template Linking Template Transitive Template Direct/Indirect Object Template Object/Objective Complement Template	Intransitive Template Linking Template Transitive Template Direct/Indirect Object Template Object/Objective Complement Template

1. _____

2. _____

3. _____

4. _____

5. _____

II. Write your own paragraph of three or four sentences, and then end it with an adverb clause fragment for emphasis.

_____

_____

_____

_____

III. Carefully read this famous sentence from Herman Melville's *Moby-Dick*, and then answer the questions that follow it.

> *Though* in many natural objects, whiteness refiningly enhances beauty, as if imparting some special virtue of its own, as in marbles, japonicas, and pearls; and *though* various nations have in some way recognised a certain royal pre-eminence in this hue; even the barbaric, grand old kings of Pegu placing the title "Lord of the White Elephants" above all their other magniloquent ascriptions of dominion; and the modern kings of Siam unfurling the same snow-white quadruped in the royal standard; and the Hanoverian flag bearing the one figure of a snow-white charger; and the great Austrian Empire, Caesarian, heir to overlording Rome, having for the imperial color the same imperial hue; and *though* this pre-eminence in it applies to the human race itself, giving the white man ideal mastership over every dusky tribe; and *though*, besides all this, whiteness has been even made significant of gladness, for among the Romans a white stone marked a joyful day; and *though* in other mortal sympathies and symbolizings, this same hue is made the emblem of many touching, noble things—the innocence of brides, the benignity of age; *though* among the Red Men of America the giving of the white belt of wampum was the deepest pledge of honor; *though* in many climes, whiteness typifies the majesty of Justice in the ermine of the Judge, and contributes to the daily state of kings and queens drawn by milk-white steeds; *though* even in the higher mysteries of the most august religions it has been made the symbol of the divine spotlessness and power; by the Persian fire worshippers, the white forked flame being held the holiest on the altar; and in the Greek mythologies, Great Jove himself made incarnate in a snow-white bull; and *though* to the noble Iroquois, the midwinter sacrifice of the sacred White Dog was by far the holiest festival of their theology, that spotless, faithful creature being held the purest envoy they could send to the Great Spirit with the annual tidings of their own fidelity; and *though* directly from the Latin word for white, all Christian priests derive the name of one part of their sacred vesture, the alb or tunic, worn beneath the cassock; and *though* among the holy pomps of the Romish faith, white is specially employed in the celebration of the Passion of our Lord; *though* in the Vision of St. John, white robes are given to the redeemed, and the four-and-twenty elders stand clothed in white before the great white throne, and the Holy One that sitteth there white like wool; yet for all these accumulated associations, with whatever is sweet, and honorable, and sublime, there yet lurks an elusive something in the innermost idea of this hue, which strikes more of panic to the soul than that redness which affrights in blood.

[Note: You may notice that these adverb clauses themselves are syntactically complex, containing a variety of modifiers such as prepositional phrases, participial phrases, and adjective clauses (covered in the next chapter). You might question whether it is right to call all of this one sentence, but one sentence it is, even at a length of almost 500 words. Here it is useful to point out that a sentence's length alone does not make it a **run-on** sentence. A run-on sentence is one that improperly combines two independent clauses without proper punctuation. This sentence does not do that. Note also that the italics are not in the original.]

Now answer the following questions:

1. How many adverb clauses do you see?

_____

2. What conjunction introduces each one?

_____

3. What is the independent clause?

_____

4. What do the adverb clauses have in common?

_____

5. How does the independent clause contradict them?

_____

IV. Write your own sentence beginning with three adverb clauses followed by an independent clause.

_____

CHAPTER NINE

Dependent Clause Templates II: Adjective Clauses

The second of the three dependent clause templates that we cover is the adjective clause.

Adjective Clauses and Relative Pronouns

You saw in the previous chapter that adverb clauses function as adverbs: they modify the same constituents, specifically independent clauses, as other adverbs do. In a similar fashion, adjective clauses function in the same way as one-word or phrase-length adjectives: they modify nouns or pronouns. However, there is a significant syntactic difference between adverb clauses and adjective clauses, beyond the fact that they modify different constituents. Whereas adverb clauses are highly movable within their templates, adjective clauses are not. Adjective clauses almost always follow the noun or pronoun that they modify. This fact causes some interesting syntactic patterns that will be discussed below. For now, let us just say that this positioning of adjective clauses frequently disrupts the usual subject-verb pattern of English clauses.

In the previous chapter, you saw that adverb clauses modify the entire independent clause with which they are associated, and that they generally do not break the syntactic flow of the independent clause. Adjective clauses, on the other hand, frequently do just that. Because they follow the noun or pronoun they modify, they will appear wherever that noun is. For example, if the noun is the subject, the adjective clause will follow it and precede the verb:

Jack, <u>who was an energetic boy</u>, trotted up the hill.

Here the independent clause is *Jack trotted up the hill*, while the adjective clause is *who was an energetic boy*. The adjective clause comes immediately after the noun subject *Jack* and precedes the verb *trotted*, which is connected to that subject. Showing this sentence in symbolic form reveals its syntax:

$$S \quad s \quad v \quad sc \quad V \quad PP.$$

The independent clause, represented by upper-case abbreviations, is shown to be an intransitive verb template beginning with a subject (S), followed by a verb (V), and then a prepositional phrase. The adjective clause on the other hand, represented by lower-case abbreviations, is a linking verb template beginning with a subject (s), followed by a verb (v), and then a subjective complement (sc). Thus, you see two subjects (S and s) right next to each other because the second is the subject of the verb in the adjective clause.

The fact that adjective clauses follow immediately after the noun or pronoun they modify produces another syntactic oddity. Adjective clauses are often introduced by **relative pronouns**, which connect the adjective clause (sometimes called a relative clause) to the specific noun or pronoun being modified. Since these connecting words are pronouns, they function in their own clause as subjects or objects. When they are an object, they still occur right after the noun or pronoun being modified:

Jack is the boy whom Jill admires.

Here the relative pronoun *whom* both introduces the adjective clause and functions as the object of the verb *admires* in that clause. Phrasing this adjective clause in more normal word order would look like this:

Jill admires whom.

That, of course, sounds odd, but only until you realize that the relative pronoun is serving as a substitute for *the boy*:

Jill admires the boy.

Using the symbolic representation as we did above produces the following:

$$S \quad V \quad SC \quad o \quad s \quad v.$$

The independent clause is a linking verb template beginning with the subject (S), followed by the verb (V), and then the subjective complement (SC). The adjective clause is a transitive verb template beginning with the object of the verb (o), followed by the subject (s), and then the verb (v).

English does not usually permit beginning a transitive verb template with an object, but in the case of adjective clauses it is quite usual. English does permit, as well, leaving out the relative pronoun:

> Jack is the boy Jill admires.

Doing that removes the oddity of beginning the transitive verb template with the object, but it also leaves out that object. (Also, note that when the relative pronoun is the subject of the adjective clause it cannot be omitted.) These syntactic oddities are responsible for a number of usage issues that will be discussed later in this chapter.

Since adjective clauses follow nouns and pronouns, one way to organize the possible positions of these clauses is to sort them by the function of the words they **modify**, i.e., add more information to. Nouns and pronouns typically function as subjects and objects. First, however, we need to examine some of the other connecting words that are used aside from relative pronouns.

Other Connecting Words

So far the examples have employed relative pronouns to introduce adjective clauses. There are two other possibilities: **relative adverbs** and **relative adjectives**. Each can introduce an adjective clause and then function as either an adjective or adverb in that clause:

> Relative adverb: Jack found the bucket <u>where</u> he left it.

The relative adverb *where* introduces the adjective clause *where he left it* and functions as an adverb in that clause. As you saw with relative pronouns, the relative adverb immediately follows the noun the adjective clause modifies. In this case, it follows *bucket*. And, again as you saw before, this syntactic demand leads to unusual word order. Here the relative adverb *where* appears at the beginning of the adjective clause before the subject *he*. More usual syntax would have the adverb at the end of the clause:

> he left it where

As we did earlier, when dealing with relative pronouns, we can replace *where* with a more typical adverb and produce a very normal sounding clause:

> he left it there

It is clear, then, that the relative adverb replaces, in this case, an adverb indicating place. Other relative adverbs refer to time and include *when, after,* and *before*:

<blockquote>
Sunday is the day <u>when</u> they rest.
They remembered the time <u>after</u> they fell down the hill.
In the days <u>before</u> they became bucket carriers, life was easier.
</blockquote>

In the last example, the adjective clause *before they became bucket carriers* follows and modifies *days*, the noun object of the prepositional phrase *in the days*. Adjective clauses follow and modify nouns wherever the nouns occur.

Relative adjectives introduce adjective clauses and function as adjective modifiers in those clauses. The most usual form for a relative adjective is *whose*.

<blockquote>
Jill remembered the girl <u>whose</u> brother introduced her to Jack.
</blockquote>

The syntax of the adjective clause in this instance is more usual because the relative *whose* modifies the subject *brother* of the adjective clause, in a typical position for adjectives, i.e., before the noun:

<blockquote>
<u>Whose</u> brother introduced her to Jack
is very similar to
<u>Her</u> brother introduced her to Jack.
</blockquote>

Let's now move on to examining the ways in which adjective clauses modify both subjects and objects.

Adjective Clauses Modifying Subjects

Subject in an intransitive template:

<blockquote>
Jack, <u>who was tired</u>, walked slowly up the hill.
</blockquote>

The adjective clause *who was tired* follows and modifies the subject *Jack* of the independent clause.

Subject in a linking verb template:

<blockquote>
Their bucket, <u>which was quite old</u>, was leaky.
</blockquote>

The adjective clause *which was quite old* follows the subject *bucket* of the independent clause.

Subject in a transitive verb template:

The rain, <u>which came suddenly</u>, splattered Jack's feet.

The adjective clause *which came suddenly* follows and modifies the subject *rain* of the independent clause. In this case, a relative pronoun introduced the adjective clause.

Subject in a direct/indirect object template:

The carpenter, <u>who was new in town</u>, gave Jack and Jill a new bucket.

The adjective clause *who was new in town* follows and modifies the subject *carpenter* of the independent clause.

Subject in an objective complement template:

The leaky bucket <u>that their parents had given them</u> made their job difficult.

The adjective clause *that their parents had given them* follows and modifies the subject *bucket* of the independent clause.

You can probably see that not only do the kinds of independent clause in which adjective clauses occur vary, but so do the templates of the adjective clauses themselves. For example, the adjective clause in the last example is in a direct/indirect object template, shown below in a more normal word order:

Their parents had given them that.

This will be clearer if we replace the relative *that* with the noun it replaces:

Their parents had given them the leaky bucket.

Or to take one more, somewhat simpler example, the adjective clause in the first illustrative sentence above is in a linking verb template:

Who was tired.

Again replacing the relative *who* with the word it replaces yields the following:

Jack was tired.

Adjective Clauses Modifying Objects

Direct object of the verb:

Jill paid the bill, <u>which was due</u>.

The adjective clause *which was due* follows and modifies *bill*, the noun object of the verb *paid* in the independent clause. The relative pronoun *which* introduces the adjective clause.

Object of a preposition:

Jill saw a hole in the bucket <u>that they carried</u>.

The adjective clause *that they carried* follows and modifies *bucket*, the noun object of the preposition *in*.

Indirect object in a direct/indirect template:

Jack gave the carpenter, <u>whose work was excellent</u>, his fee.

The adjective clause *whose work was excellent* follows and modifies *carpenter*, the indirect noun object of *gave*. The relative adjective *whose* introduces the adjective clause.

Direct object in a direct/indirect template:

Jill gave all the money <u>that she had</u> to the carpenter for his bill.

The adjective clause *that she had* follows and modifies *money* the direct object of *gave*.

Noun objective complement:

Jack and Jill considered their job a responsibility <u>that served their community</u>.

The adjective clause *that served their community* follows and modifies the noun objective complement *responsibility*.

The Basic Templates

Because of the complexity and variety of syntactic possibilities in which adjective clauses can occur, these possibilities can only be represented broadly. The illustrations below show the position of adjective clauses following the subject of the independent clause, following the object (direct or indirect) of the independent clause, and following the object of a prepositional phrase. As you can see, wherever the adjective clause occurs, it follows the noun or pronoun that it modifies and cannot be moved from that position without rewording the sentence.

After a Subject

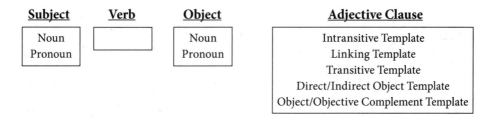

After Object of a Verb

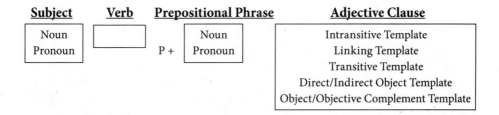

After Object of a Preposition

These illustrations are only some of the numerous possibilities. For example, the last illustration shows an intransitive template with a prepositional phrase after the verb, and then the adjective clause, which modifies the object of that preposition. But since prepositional phrases can occur anywhere in any template, you can imagine how many other possibilities there are. Note as well that in these examples as throughout the chapter only nouns and pronouns have been shown because they are the most common constituents. However, it is possible for an adjective clause to modify gerunds and infinitives, as they are noun substitutes. You will have an opportunity to work with some of the possibilities not specifically illustrated above.

Matters of Style

Adjective clauses modify nouns or pronouns. Modification means adding details that paint a fuller picture of whatever is being modified. Thus, when a noun subject occurs early in a sentence, readers wait to find out what that subject did or what they will learn about the subject. Placing an adjective clause after that noun, but before the information readers expect, creates anticipation. And, as you have seen before, creating that tension can be stylistically effective.

To illustrate let's start with a famous saying, taking it word by word. It begins with the pronoun *he*. Since we are dealing with a pronoun, we have to establish that in this case there is no antecedent (i.e., a noun to which the pronoun refers). Readers encountering this saying would first see

He

Because there is no antecedent, the pronoun likely refers to a generic person, and because this saying originated before concerns of sexism in the language would proscribe its usage, it is in the masculine gender representing all possible persons. And because *he* is in the nominative case, readers immediately understand that it is the subject of a clause. Readers accustomed to typical English syntax would anticipate a verb appearing next in the sentence.

But instead, readers encounter the following:

He who

This next word, far from being the anticipated verb, is instead another pronoun—in this case a relative pronoun—in the nominative case. Readers now entertain two thoughts about where this sentence is going. First, seeing the relative pronoun alerts readers to the probability that an adjective clause is beginning, even if they do not know the technical term for it. They expect that clause to offer some additional information about the subject; that is, they will know something more about this generic *he*. Second, because of the nominative case of the relative pronoun, readers again expect it to be followed by a verb.

This time, their expectation turns out to be correct:

He who laughs last

Now readers know that the subject of this sentence, the generic person, is the one who in situations that prompt laughter is the one who has the last laugh. But, consciously or not, readers await the verb to attach to *he*, the subject of the independent clause with which the sentence begins. They now get that verb:

He who laughs last laughs

All of the weight of this sentence now falls on readers' expectation for the word that will follow the verb. For example, a person can laugh last in a mocking fashion, crowing over a beaten opponent to punctuate the victory. That does not, however, appear to be exactly the case, as this sentence finishes with the adverb *best*, adding to, and emphasizing, the meaning of the previous adverb *last*: The laugh of the generic person is not only last but most satisfying.

He who laughs last laughs best.

This walk through the adjective clause in this well-known saying (the line can be traced back to *Christmas Prince*, a seventeenth century English play) illustrates how an adjective clause can be utilized to stylistic advantage. In this case, the effect is enhanced by sound: the repetition of the initial *l* is a poetic technique called "alliteration," while the repetition of the vowel sound is termed "assonance." There's also a variant of the saying that uses *longest* instead of *best*, thus making the alliteration even more pronounced.

As you can see, the stylistic value is based on creating an expectation that will be addressed on the other side of the adjective clause. Readers encounter a subject, but instead of the expected verb they see the start of another clause that will add to or modify their sense of the initial subject. Then, after that additional information is presented, they see the verb that attaches to that subject, followed by the rest of the template of the independent clause.

Let's try one example of our own devising:

Jack

Add one adjective clause after the subject:

Jack, who was feeling lucky

Now another:

Jack, who was feeling lucky, and who had money in his pocket

One more:

Jack, who was feeling lucky, who had money in his pocket, and who was whistling a happy tune

At this point, readers will still be waiting for the verb that will attach to the original subject. What might it be? What template will it introduce?

Here's one possibility:

> Jack, who was feeling lucky, who had money in his pocket, and who was whistling a happy tune, strode into the casino.

In this case, the completion of the independent clause template is satisfying because it reinforces the information contained in the adjective clauses. It is equally possible, of course, for that completion of the independent clause to undercut or contradict, to change the direction that the clauses had established. You will have an opportunity to work with such possibilities in the exercises.

Matters of Usage

The syntactic necessity of adjective clauses following the noun or pronoun they modify creates several usage issues. Chief among these is the case—nominative or objective—of the relative pronoun that often introduces these clauses. In addition, in formal situations a careful distinction is demanded between what are called **restrictive** and **non-restrictive** clauses. Finally, a relic of early English grammarians to subject English to Latin grammar produces the prohibition against ending a sentence with a preposition.

Relative Pronoun Case

In English, as we have seen, pronouns change form for case, while nouns do not. Here's a quick reminder of how this change of form works:

> He saw him.

Here the first pronoun *he* is in the nominative case because it is functioning as a subject, while the second pronoun *him* is in the objective case because it is the object of the verb *saw*. In contrast, nouns do not change to reflect function:

> The boy saw the girl.
> The girl saw the boy.

Although the two nouns switch between being subject and object in these sentences, their form does not change.

Similarly, the relative pronoun *who* is in the nominative case, while *whom* is in the objective case. These pronouns introduce adjective clauses and function within those clauses as either a subject or an object. What complicates the issue is the fact that the relative pronoun, as you saw above (p. 129), always comes immediately after the noun or pronoun being modified and therefore appears at the beginning of the clause. This fact causes little confusion when the relative pronoun is functioning as a subject:

Jack looked for the carpenter <u>who</u> fixed the bucket.

Here *who* introduces the adjective clause and functions as the subject of the verb *fixed* of that clause. As such, it appears before the verb, as usually happens in English syntax.

However, look at a sentence in which the relative pronoun functions as an object of the verb in its clause:

Jill looked for the carpenter <u>whom</u> Jack recommended.

Here *whom* is in the objective case because it is the object of the verb *recommended*. It comes first in the adjective clause because that's what relative pronouns must do, here providing a direct object preceding both the subject *Jack* and the verb *recommended* of the clause.

Most people do not have a problem with starting the clause with the relative pronoun. In fact, English insists that you do that. But that position at the beginning of the clause encourages people to use the nominative form even when the objective case is demanded by the function of the pronoun in its own clause. Therefore, for the sentence above it would not be unusual to hear or read:

Jill looked for the carpenter who Jack recommended.

How unusual that sounds depends upon the level of usage you customarily encounter. However, in relatively formal situations there is a clear preference for the grammatically appropriate case of the pronoun.

The key to figuring out the preferred choice in such sentences is to determine what the relative pronoun is doing in its own clause. Is it the subject of the verb or is it the verb's object? Often you will have to reword the clause to put it into more usual word order, such that it starts with the subject. Focusing on the verb helps you see what its subject is and you can go on from there. Another technique is to drop the relative pronoun—if it can be dropped, it's an object, since subject pronouns can't be omitted.

Restrictive and Non-Restrictive Clauses

Adjective clauses modify nouns or pronouns. In more formal usage, a distinction is drawn between clauses that identify the noun or pronoun being modified and those that simply add information to an entity whose identity is clear. Those clauses that identify are termed **restrictive**, as in the following example:

Jill remembered the hill <u>that they first walked up</u>.

Here the adjective clause identifies which hill Jane is remembering. Of all the possible hills, she is talking about the one that she and Jack first walked up to fetch their pail of water. Therefore, this clause is restrictive because it identifies a specific hill.

On the other hand, clauses that provide additional information to an entity already clearly identified are termed **non-restrictive**, as in the following:

Jill recalled Brown's Hill, <u>which they first walked up</u>.

Here the adjective clause adds additional information to a hill that is already identified by its proper name.

Of course, proper nouns make the distinction simple, since they clearly establish what or who is being talked about. In other instances, the distinction is a bit less obvious:

Jack met his best friend, who was also on his way to town.

In this case, even without the name of the friend, readers can see that of all Jack's friends, this sentence refers to the best one. Therefore, the clause that follows is non-restrictive.

The only reason for distinguishing between these two kinds of clauses is because formal usage underscores the distinction in two ways, as you might have noticed: first, non-restrictive clauses are preceded by a comma while restrictive clauses are not; and second, when referring to non-human antecedents (as in the hill example above), restrictive clauses employ the relative pronoun *that*, while non-restrictive clauses use *which*. However, when the antecedent for the relative pronoun in a non-restrictive clause is human, the use of *which* does not sound correct:

Jill respected Jack, which she met a long time ago.

Clearly, *that* doesn't work much better:

Jill respected Jack, that she met a long time ago.

What sounds best is the following:

Jill respected Jack, whom she met a long time ago.

For human antecedents, choosing between *who* or *whom*, depending on case, for non-restrictive situations is preferred. For restrictive adjective clauses dealing with humans, the choice is between *who/whom* and *that*:

Jack found the old acquaintance *that* he had not seen in years.
Jack found the old acquaintance *whom* he had not seen in years.

The clause in each case is restrictive, telling us which of all of Jack's old acquaintances he found. The *whom* version sounds more formal, but *that* is acceptable at a lesser level of formality, while *which* would clearly be inappropriate.

Whether to extend this distinction to people's pets is a question beyond the scope of this discussion.

Ending a Sentence (or Clause) with a Preposition

In the seventeenth and eighteenth centuries, formal usage in English had not yet been established. Some self-appointed guardians of the language stepped forward and decided that classical Latin was the model for a civilized language and therefore proposed a number of usage rules emulating those found in Latin. Among these was Latin's insistence that a preposition must precede its object. Even the etymology of the term itself reflects this idea: Latin *prae* and *ponere*, meaning "to place before." Thus a preposition must, in Latin, come before its object.

Clearly, however, English is not Latin. Its original source is Germanic Anglo-Saxon (Old English), to which has been added large doses of French after England was conquered by the Norman French in 1066, and later Greek and Latin during the focus on classical languages during the Renaissance. To impose Latin grammar on English simply makes no sense.

And yet it was done and continues to create misguided "rules," such as the one under discussion.

Among the instances where this rule can be seen is in adjective clauses that begin with a relative pronoun as the object of a preposition.

Jill bought the new best seller, which Jack asked her for.

Putting that adjective clause into more usual English word order yields the following:

Jack asked her for which.

Again, as we have done before, replace the relative with its personal pronoun alternative:

Jack asked her for it.

Substituting *it* for *which* reveals the syntax of the clause without changing it.

Applying the Latin-based rule, this sentence would be constructed this way:

Jill bought the book for which Jack asked her.

Here the preposition *for* is placed before its object *which* to create the prepositional phrase *for which*. If this sounds more formal to you, that impression is understandable. Formal usage sometimes does prefer this alternative, which is fine as long as you understand it as a stylistic rather than a usage preference. In that regard, a stylistic argument for this usage could be that a preposition at the end of a sentence deprives that ending of emphasis; prepositions are not by their nature strong words. The trade-off is that the more formal version seems a little dated and unnatural. Both, however, are equally acceptable.

Exercises

I. Sentences with Adjective Clauses

A. Using one of the template choices for the adjective clause that modifies the *subject* in an *intransitive* template, compose three sentences. Indicate which template has been employed for the adjective clause.

Subject	Adjective Clause	Verb
Noun Pronoun	Intransitive Template Linking Template Transitive Template Direct/Indirect Object Template Object/Objective Complement Template	

1. _____

Adjective Clause Template:_____

2. _____

Adjective Clause Template:_____

3. _____

Adjective Clause Template:_____

B. Now, using one of the template choices for the adjective clause that modifies the *object* in a *transitive* template, compose three sentences. Indicate which template has been employed for the adjective clause.

Subject	Verb	Object	Adjective Clause
Noun Pronoun		Noun Pronoun	Intransitive Template Linking Template Transitive Template Direct/Indirect Object Template Object/Objective Complement Template

1. _____

Adjective Clause Template:_____

2. _____

Adjective Clause Template:_____

3. _____

Adjective Clause Template:_____

C. Next, using one of the template choices for the adjective clause that modifies the *subject* in a *linking verb* template, compose three sentences. Indicate which template has been employed for the adjective clause.

Subject	Adjective Clause	Verb	Subjective Complement
Noun Pronoun	Intransitive Template Linking Template Transitive Template Direct/Indirect Object Template Object/Objective Complement Template		Noun Pronoun Adjective

1. _____

Adjective Clause Template:_____

2. _____

Adjective Clause Template:_____

3. _____

Adjective Clause Template:_____

D. Now, using one of the template choices for the adjective clause that modifies the *object of a preposition* in an *intransitive* template, compose three sentences. Indicate which template has been employed for the adjective clause.

Subject	Verb	Prepositional Phrase	Adjective Clause
Noun Pronoun		P + Noun Pronoun	Intransitive Template Linking Template Transitive Template Direct/Indirect Object Template Object/Objective Complement Template

1. _____

Adjective Clause Template:_____

2. _____

Adjective Clause Template:_____

3. _____

Adjective Clause Template:_____

E. Compose a sentence with at least two consecutive adjective clauses modifying a subject in any template.

_____

F. Compose a sentence with at least two consecutive adjective clauses modifying an object in any template. The object can be that of a verb or a preposition.

_____

II. Usage Matters

Identify the usage issues you see in the following sentences. If there is no issue, write a C (for correct) in the space provided.

1. That is the man who Jack saw at the top of the hill.

Usage Issue:_____

2. Jill finished reading *Moby-Dick* that her teacher assigned.

Usage Issue:_____

3. Jack also read *Moby-Dick*, which he found to be too long.

Usage Issue:_____

4. Jack and Jill, whom were well known by everyone in town, decided to open a business.

Usage Issue:_____

5. Jack and Jill, who thought they knew everyone in town, decided to open a business.

Usage Issue:_____

CHAPTER TEN

Dependent Clause Templates III: Noun Clauses

The last type of dependent clause to be examined is the one in which the clause does the job of individual noun phrases. Simply put, a **noun clause** takes the place of a noun or noun phrase. That means that these clauses will always be embedded in a larger structure, just as nouns are. This feature contrasts sharply with adverb and adjective clauses, as those are separate syntactic structures, set apart from the independent clause to which they are attached. Noun clauses, on the other hand, are always found as *part of* another clause.

Noun clauses add a great deal of flexibility and complexity to English syntax. Because noun clauses function syntactically in the same places where a noun can appear, they can be found as subjects or objects of verbs, as objects of prepositions, and as subjective or objective complements. In each case, the noun clause will be in its own template, with its own subject and verb and whatever other constituents are called for by the particular template.

The following words typically introduce noun clauses: *that, if, whether, where, when, who,* and *why.* This list includes conjunctions (*that, if, whether*), relative pronouns (*what, who*), relative adjectives (*which, whose*), and relative adverbs (*where, when*).

Noun Clauses

Let's begin by looking at how noun clauses are structured and the places where they can occur.

Noun clause as subject of a verb:

<u>That Jack works hard</u> is obvious.

The noun clause *that Jack works hard* is the subject of the verb *is* in a linking verb template:

Subject	Linking Verb	Subjective Complement
That Jack works hard	is	obvious.

You can probably already note one of the qualities of this kind of construction, namely how frontloaded the sentence is, with a clause containing its own subject and verb sitting in the necessary subject slot of another clause. This structural quality will be further discussed later in this chapter when we look at stylistic matters.

In a related sense, and perhaps because of this front-heavy feel, English offers a smoother way to say the same thing:

<u>It</u> is obvious <u>that Jack works hard</u>.

Grammarians analyzing this kind of sentence call the *it* in the subject slot a "syntactic expletive," a word that occupies grammatical space but does not communicate anything. Here the word occupies the subject slot but does not communicate any meaning. Rather, the word satisfies our need to have something that could be a subject in that slot. Placing *it* in the subject slot delays the entrance of the meaningful subject until the end of the sentence where the noun clause appears; it also enables the verb of the independent clause, in this case *is*, to follow immediately after the subject.

Besides occupying the subject slot in templates, noun clauses also show up as objects of verbs:

Jill knows <u>that Jack works hard</u>.

In this case, the same noun clause *that Jack works hard* is now seen as the direct object of the verb *knows*:

Subject	Verb	Object
Jill	knows	that Jack works hard.

Jill knows something, and in this case that something is the fact that Jack works hard.

Note that changing the conjunction *that* to other introductory words alters the meaning:

Jill knows <u>when</u> Jack works hard.
Jill knows <u>where</u> Jack works hard.
Jill knows <u>why</u> Jack works hard.
Jill knows <u>whether</u> Jack works hard.

In each example, Jill knows something else about Jack's working; however, grammatically each noun clause is still the direct object of the verb *knows*.

Noun clauses can also appear as subjective complements in a linking verb template, usually after a form of *be*:

Jack's problem is <u>that he is tired of walking up that hill</u>.

Here, the noun clause *that he is tired of walking up that hill* is introduced by the subordinating conjunction *that* and serves as the subjective complement of *is* in a linking verb template.

The third place where noun clauses commonly occur is as objects of prepositions. This possibility might initially seem rather odd, since we ordinarily think of prepositional phrases as simple syntactic structures composed of a preposition and its object. But since nouns or noun equivalents are always the object of prepositions, and because noun clauses can take the place of nouns, we encounter sentences such as this:

Jill worried about <u>what the day would bring</u>.

In this intransitive template the prepositional phrase *about what the day would bring* modifies the verb *worried*. And the object of the preposition *about* is the noun clause *what the day would bring*:

Subject	Verb	Preposition	Object
Jill	worried	about	what the day would bring.

The noun clause object begins with the relative pronoun *what*, which is the object of the clause's verb *would bring*:

Object	Subject	Verb
what	the day	would bring

Put into more ordinary word order the clause reads this way:

Subject	Verb	Object
the day	would bring	what

Finally, as we did before, replacing the relative pronoun with the pronoun *that* sounds better:

The day	would bring	that.

A common variety of noun clauses serving as objects, either of a verb or of a preposition, begins with the relative pronoun *whoever*:

Jack looked for <u>whoever could help repair his leaky bucket</u>.

You might guess at this point that this kind of noun clause object can pose a usage problem, because, as with *who* and *whom*, *whoever* has an object equivalent *whomever*, and a choice needs to be made between these two depending upon whether or not the pronoun is a subject or object in its own clause. This is a matter discussed in the usage section. For now, we can note that in the example above, *whoever* is the subject of the verb *could help*; the object of the preposition is the entire noun clause.

Less commonly than the above examples, noun clauses can be found in these additional noun function slots:

Indirect Object: Jack gave <u>whoever saw him</u> a friendly smile.

The noun clause *whoever saw him* is the indirect object, while *a friendly smile* is the direct object.

Apposition: Jill remembers the important fact, <u>that Jack is an ambitious water carrier</u>.

The noun clause *that Jack is an ambitious water carrier* is in apposition to *fact*.
This final example is of an even less common structure:

Objective Complement: Jack considered his pail <u>what carpenters thought of their hammers</u>.

The clause *what carpenters thought of their hammers* is the objective complement, while *his pail* is the direct object.

These last are included for the sake of completeness, but we will concentrate on the first three, more common, places where noun clauses occur. How we can illustrate those situations is outlined in the next section. Because of the syntactic complexity of noun clauses, example sentences are provided in the following illustrations.

The Basic Templates

Noun Clause as Subject

Noun Clause	**Verb**
Intransitive Template Linking Template Transitive Template Direct/Indirect Object Template Object/Objective Complement Template	

That Jack works hard   matters.

Noun Clause Subject with Expletive It

It	**Verb**	**Noun Clause**
		Intransitive Template Linking Template Transitive Template Direct/Indirect Object Template Object/Objective Complement Template

It   matters   that Jack works hard.

Noun Clause as Subjective Complement

Subject	**Verb**	**Subjective Complement**
		Intransitive Template Linking Template Transitive Template Direct/Indirect Object Template Object/Objective Complement Template

Jill   became   what her life offered.

Noun Clause Object of the Verb

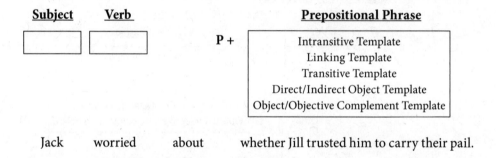

Subject	Verb	Noun Clause
		Intransitive Template Linking Template Transitive Template Direct/Indirect Object Template Object/Objective Complement Template
Jill	believes	that Jack works hard.

Noun Clause Object of a Preposition

Subject	Verb		Prepositional Phrase
		P +	Intransitive Template Linking Template Transitive Template Direct/Indirect Object Template Object/Objective Complement Template
Jack	worried	about	whether Jill trusted him to carry their pail.

As noted in the previous chapters, these illustrations are intended to be only suggestive of the many possibilities that English syntax offers.

Matters of Style

As has been the theme of these sections of the book, effective style works with the expectations that templates create. As readers begin to process a sentence, their minds anticipate the shape they expect the template to take. Effective style either confirms this expectation by producing the usual syntax, or varies from that in a way that causes a tension, an uncertainty, as readers now want to know what surprise is in order.

For example, beginning a sentence with a noun clause has the effect of creating an expectation that the end of the sentence is going to be particularly important. This is so because the noun clause in the subject slot provides so much more information than the ordinary noun or noun phrase that readers expect a reward at the end of the sentence, something to balance the relative heaviness of the beginning.

Let's see how that works. Here is a substantial noun clause at the beginning of a sentence:

That Jack and Jill worked so well together despite their earlier misadventure...

This clause contains a lot of information. The subordinating conjunction *that* alerts readers to the fact that this clause, with its own subject and verb, adverb modifiers, and prepositional phrase occupies the subject slot of some template. Accordingly, readers getting to the end of this clause await a verb. Let's add one:

> That Jack and Jill worked so well together despite their earlier
> misadventure <u>surprised</u>...

The sentence has now created considerable anticipation. What will follow the verb? It is a transitive verb, so readers, recognizing that, want to know what the verb's object will tell them. Two obvious choices are *no one* or *everyone*:

> That Jack and Jill worked so well together despite their earlier
> misadventure surprised <u>no one</u>.
> That Jack and Jill worked so well together despite their earlier
> misadventure surprised <u>everyone</u>.

Context would dictate the choice between these alternatives. And finally, adding an adjective clause to modify the pronoun would provide some emphasis. Here is how that would look:

> That Jack and Jill worked so well together despite their earlier misadventure
> surprised no one <u>who knew them</u>.

A similar stylistic effect is produced by the expletive *it*, which usually begins a linking verb template such as the following:

> It is clear...

Although these three words create a grammatically complete clause, that clause doesn't tell us very much. That is because the pronoun *it*, without an antecedent, means literally nothing or everything. Readers at this point will want to know exactly what "is clear." The answer to that question arrives in the form of the noun clause that is the actual subject of the sentence. Taking the noun clause from the previous example produces the following:

> It is clear <u>that Jack and Jill work so well together despite their</u>
> <u>previous misadventure</u>.

In the previous example, readers would want to know what object follows the verb *surprises*. In this illustration, the adjective *clear* is what creates the anticipation. Different adjectives, such as *unusual* or *natural* or *plausible*, among many possibilities, can replace *clear*, each generating a question that the noun clause will answer. The choice of whether to place a noun clause at the beginning of the sentence, or to delay it using an *it* construction, leads to very different stylistic effects that will depend on your intentions as a writer.

As you gain more control of the templates presented in this text, you will be able to work toward greater stylistic emphasis. For example, one way to create emphasis is through repetition. Think way back to the examples of song structure in the first chapter (p. 16). There you saw how certain musical patterns were repeated so that listeners very quickly come to recognize those repetitions and to anticipate the patterns. In songs, these musical patterns contain lyrics; thus it is possible to have a contrast between the identical musical notes on the one hand, and the different words contained in the lyrics on the other. That is what happens in the *AABA* song structure. In the verse-chorus structure, again the musical patterns repeat. The lyrics in the verses differ from each other, but those in the chorus repeat.

Writers use similar techniques. Perhaps John F. Kennedy's most well-remembered lines come from his first inaugural address:

> My fellow Americans: ask not what your country can do for you—ask what you can do for your country.

After the introductory phrase, the sentence presents two direct/indirect object templates in the form of **imperatives**, or commands. The language in these two templates is almost identical. With the exception of the adverb *not* in the first template, the words are the same. What changes is the order.

In each template, the verb is *ask*, followed by a noun clause in this pattern:

Direct Object	Subject	Verb	Indirect Object
what	your country	can do	for you
what	you	can do	for your country

The two noun clauses are identical in structure, a technique known as parallel structure. What shift places from one to the other are the subject and the indirect object. The fact that exactly the same words and syntactic structure are used produces very strong stylistic emphasis.

Formal speeches such as this one are good places to look for examples of this kind of careful structuring. The rest of Kennedy's speech contains a number of such applications of stylistic repetition and contrast.

Let's look at one more example of a skilled writer's stylistic use of a noun clause, this time as the object of a verbal rather than a verb. In the following excerpt from seventeenth-century English poet John Donne's *Meditation 17*, the noun clause object of the verb *to know* (indicated in italics below) has been adopted by many writers and artists, from Ernest Hemingway for the title of a novel, to the heavy-metal band Metallica for one of their tunes.

No man is an island, entire of itself; every man is a piece of the continent, a part of the main. If a clod be washed away by the sea, Europe is the less, as well as if a promontory were, as well as if a manor of thy friend's or of thine own were: any man's death diminishes me, because I am involved in mankind, and therefore never send to know *for whom the bells tolls*; it tolls for thee.

Similar to the Kennedy example above, the independent clause beginning with *therefore* is in the imperative (command) mood with an understood subject. As noted above, the noun clause is the object of the verbal (*to know*):

Subject	Adverb	Verb	Verbal	Noun Clause Object
(You)	never	send	to know	for whom the bell tolls

In this case, the prepositional phrase *for whom* starts the noun clause, and the pronoun is in the objective case as it is the object of the preposition. Rewording the noun clause into usual subject/verb syntax and substituting a pronoun in the objective case for *whom* produces the following:

the bell tolls for him (or her or them)

Donne's choice for a substitute pronoun in the objective case appears in the concluding clause: it tolls for *thee*.

You might also want to examine the Donne passage above for examples of repetition and parallel structure.

Matters of Usage

The main usage concern in noun clauses is the case of the relative pronouns that so frequently introduce them. In this respect, as you saw in the previous chapter (pp. 138–39), these problems are similar to those that occur in adjective clauses, which are also introduced by relative pronouns. In both templates, the relative pronoun that begins the clause is not necessarily the subject of the verb that follows. In fact, in many instances, these pronouns are the object of that verb.

The following illustrates the difference between a relative pronoun introducing a noun clause as subject of the verb in that clause and one that is the object of the verb in the clause:

Subject: Jack saw <u>who</u> was talking to Jill.

Here the relative pronoun *who* is the subject of the verb phrase *was talking*. Because it is the subject, the pronoun is in the nominative case.

Object: Jill knew <u>whom</u> she could trust.

The pronoun *whom* is in the objective case because it is the object of the verb phrase *could trust*, even though it precedes that phrase.

The problem of deciding upon case is more difficult when the noun clause is the object of a preposition. That is so because when we read a preposition we expect it to be followed by an object. Therefore, relative pronouns in the objective case will almost always sound right when they introduce a noun clause object of a preposition, regardless of whether they are the subject or the object of that clause.

To see how this sentence illustrates this problem, read it word by word until you get to the preposition:

Jack looked for...

Now, if a relative pronoun follows, your ear is probably tuned to expect it to be in the objective case:

Jack looked for whomever...

So far that probably sounds good.

Jack looked for whomever could repair...

Now the problem has arisen. The sentence offers a verb phrase after the relative pronoun.

Jack looked for <u>whomever</u> could repair his leaking bucket.

Your ear might still insist that the case of the relative pronoun is acceptable; however, it is not. The pronoun introduces the noun clause object of the preposition *for*, but it also serves as the subject of the verb of that clause. Accordingly, preferred usage would have it in the nominative case:

Jack looked for <u>whoever</u> could repair his leaking bucket.

Exercises

I. Sentences with Noun Clauses

A. Using one of the templates for a noun clause as the *subject* of an *intransitive* verb template, write three sentences. Identify which template you used for the noun clause.

Noun Clause Subject	Verb
Intransitive Template Linking Template Transitive Template Direct/Indirect Object Template Object/Objective Complement Template	

1. _____

Noun Clause Template:_____

2. _____

Noun Clause Template:_____

3. _____

Noun Clause Template:_____

B. Now compose three sentences using the expletive *it* pattern in a *linking verb* template with an *adjective subjective complement*. Identify which template you used for the noun clause in the actual subject.

It subject	Linking Verb	Adjective		Noun Clause (Actual Subject)
It	is		that	Intransitive Template Linking Template Transitive Template Direct/Indirect Object Template Object/Objective Complement Template

1. _____

Noun Clause Template:_____

2. _____

Noun Clause Template:_____

3. _____

Noun Clause Template:_____

C. Next, using a form of *be* as a linking verb, write three sentences with a noun clause as the subjective complement. Indicate which template you used for the noun clause.

Subject	**Linking Verb**	**Noun Clause Subjective Complement**
Noun Pronoun	be	Intransitive Template Linking Template Transitive Template Direct/Indirect Object Template Object/Objective Complement Template

1. _____

Noun Clause Template:_____

2. _____

Noun Clause Template:_____

3. _____

Noun Clause Template:_____

D. Now compose three sentences in a *transitive verb* template using a noun clause as the *direct object* of the verb. Indicate which template you used for the noun clause.

Subject	**Transitive Verb**	**Noun Clause Direct Object**
Noun Pronoun		Intransitive Template Linking Template Transitive Template Direct/Indirect Object Template Object/Objective Complement Template

1. _____

Noun Clause Template:_____

2. _____

Noun Clause Template:_____

3. _____

Noun Clause Template:_____

E. Next, compose three sentences with noun clause objects of one of the prepositions in the drop-down menu in an *intransitive* template. Indicate which template you used for the noun clause object.

Subject	**Verb**	**Preposition**	**Noun Clause Object**
Noun Pronoun		about whether to with	Intransitive Template Linking Template Transitive Template Direct/Indirect Object Template Object/Objective Complement Template

1. _____

Noun Clause Template:_____

2. _____

Noun Clause Template:_____

3. _____

Noun Clause Template:_____

F. Compose a sentence beginning with a noun clause *subject* in a *linking verb* template such that the noun clause subject will create anticipation for what the subjective complement will say.

_____

G. Compose a sentence with an expletive *it* subject in a linking verb template and a noun clause subjective complement such that the subjective complement provides a satisfying answer to what the "it" is.

_____

H. Finally, compose a sentence with two noun clauses in the same syntactic structure such that the language in one contrasts or compares to the language in the other. Look back at the examples from Kennedy and Donne for inspiration.

_____

II. Usage Matters

Choose the correct form of the pronouns introducing noun clauses in each of the following:

1. Choose (whoever, whomever) you want.
2. (Whoever, whomever) finds the prize is the winner.
3. I was concerned about (who, whom) would be able to help me.
4. My boss told me to hire (who, whom) I thought was best qualified for the job.
5. The problem is (who, whom) will be available.

Glossary

active voice: the form of a transitive verb template in which the subject performs an action that has an effect upon the object of the transitive verb

adjective: a modifier of nouns or noun equivalents

adjective clause: a type of dependent clause; a constituent containing its own subject and verb and functioning as an adjective, that is, modifying nouns or noun equivalents; often called a relative clause

adverb: a modifier of verbs, adverbs, adjectives, prepositions, and whole clauses or sentences

adverb clause: a type of dependent clause; a constituent containing its own subject and verb and functioning as an adverb

antecedent: the noun or pronoun to which a pronoun refers (looks back to)

apposition: placed next to, as in a "noun in apposition," and typically restating in a different way the noun it is in apposition to

article: the words *a*, *an*, and *the*, placed before a noun and beginning a noun phrase, sometimes called a noun determiner because nouns always follow them

auxiliary: often called a helping verb, precedes and provides grammatical definition to a verb phrase

by **phrase:** the phrase, in the form of a prepositional phrase, in a passive form transitive verb template, containing the doer of the action (the agent)

case: the grammatical function of being either a subject or an object

clause: a constituent containing its own subject and verb

comma splice: in formal usage, a punctuation error wherein two independent clauses are combined with only a comma instead of a stronger mark of punctuation or an appropriate combining word

complex sentence: a sentence containing at least one independent clause, and one or more dependent clauses

compound: a group containing two or more equal constituents

compound object: containing two or more objects, as in "Jack saw *Jill and her cousin* on the hill."

compound sentence: a sentence containing two or more independent clauses

compound subject: containing two or more subjects, as in "*Jack and Jill* went up the hill."

conjunction: a combining word, such as *and* (coordinating) or *because* (subordinating)

conjunctive adverb: a combining word that also functions as an adverb, such as *however* or *moreover*

constituent: a word, or group of words, performing a grammatical function, or classified by formal characteristics

coordinating conjunction: a combining word connecting two constituents of equal grammatical value

dependent clause: a clause that in formal usage cannot be punctuated as its own sentence but must be attached to an independent clause

direct object: a noun, or noun equivalent, that is linked to a subject and verb in an active voice transitive verb template, in a relationship whereby the object is directly affected by the verb *do* **auxiliary:** a helping verb form used to create questions or emphasis in verb phrases

expletive *it*: *see* impersonal *it*

formal characteristics: markers of words that indicate how they should be classified, as an *-ed* suffix on verbs, or a *-ment* suffix on nouns

fragment: a group of words punctuated as a sentence but not containing its own subject and verb; a dependent clause punctuated as a sentence

gerund: a verbal formed by adding *-ing* to the base form of the verb, and functioning as a noun

imperative: in traditional grammar, a mood that expresses a command

impersonal *it*: a pronoun that fills the subject slot, but carries no real meaning; sometimes termed an expletive *it*

independent clause: a clause that can stand alone and be punctuated as a sentence

indirect object: the person or thing to which a direct object is given

infinitive: the base form of the verb as found in the dictionary, used in certain verb phrases and as a noun substitute (a verbal); usually preceded by the word *to*, as in *to walk*

inflection: a change in the form of a word to indicate a grammatical fact, such as adding an *-s* to create the third person singular of verbs

linking verb: one of a small list of English verbs that can be used in a linking verb template, the most common being *be*

main clause: *see* independent clause

modify: to change or add to the meaning of a constituent; e.g., adjectives modify nouns

mood: a quality of verbs, expressing fact (indicative mood), possibility (subjunctive mood), or command (imperative mood)

nominative case: the form of pronouns when they are being used as subjects; often called subjective case

non-restrictive: a modifier, usually an adjective clause, that adds information to but does not identify a noun or pronoun; it is separated from its antecedent by a comma

notional: a quality of definition that is dependent on meaning, such as saying "a noun is the name of a person, place or thing"

noun: a constituent defined by its function as a subject or object, and formally by its manner of forming plurals

noun clause: a type of dependent clause; a clause containing its own subject and verb but filling a noun slot in a template

noun determiner: *see* article

noun phrase: a group of words headed by a noun and functioning as a noun

number: the grammatical term that indicates whether something is singular or plural

object: *see* direct object; indirect object; object of preposition

object of preposition: a noun or noun substitute functioning as the object in a prepositional phrase

objective case: the form of a noun or pronoun when it is functioning as an object

objective complement: a noun or noun equivalent that follows a direct object and completes its meaning

participial phrase: a constituent built around either a present or past participle

participle: a form created from a verb and completing verb phrases or functioning as either noun substitutes or modifiers; *see* past participle; present participle

passive voice: the form of a transitive verb template in which the subject of the verb is acted upon

past participle: a verb form created in regular verbs by adding an -*ed* to the base form of the verb; in irregular verbs it is the form that follows in the verb phrase *I have...*

person: indicating either the speaker of an utterance (first person: *I/we*), the addressee of the utterance (second person: *you*), or the person or thing that the utterance is about (third person: *he/she/it/they*)

personal pronoun: pronouns that change form to reflect the concept of person, i.e., first person (*I, we, me, us*), second person (*you*), third person (*he, him, she, her, it, they, them*); these changes also reflect number (singular and plural), and case (subjective and objective)

phrase: a group of words that perform a particular grammatical function

preposition: the constituent that introduces a prepositional phrase (see below); often prepositions are the same words that function as single-word adverbs

prepositional phrase: a group of words beginning with a preposition and ending with an object of that preposition and functioning as a modifier

present participle: a form of a verb ending in *-ing* and functioning either as the main verb in a verb phrase or separately as a modifier

pronoun: a word that functions as and replaces a noun

relative adjective: an adjective, such as *whose*, that introduces a clause and modifies a noun or pronoun within that clause while relating back to a previous constituent (antecedent)

relative adverb: an adverb, such as *where*, that introduces a clause and functions as a modifier within that clause while relating back to a previous constituent (antecedent)

relative clause: *see* adjective clause

relative pronoun: a pronoun, such as *who* or *which*, that introduces a clause and functions as a noun equivalent within that clause while relating back to a previous constituent (antecedent)

restrictive: a modifier, usually an adjective clause, that identifies what is being modified; it is not separated from its antecedent by a comma

run-on: two or more independent clauses combined into one sentence without proper (or any) punctuation

subject: a constituent that governs a particular verb

subjective case: *see* nominative case

subjective complement: a constituent in a linking verb template that restates or modifies the subject

subordinate clause: *see* dependent clause

subordinating conjunction: a combining word that introduces a dependent clause

tense: a quality of verbs, sometimes identified with time, but more precisely classified by formal characteristics

transitional phrase: a phrase that serves to connect one idea to a preceding one

usage: a term that describes the relative formality of grammatical choices, sometimes thought of as "rules"

verb: the necessary syntactic constituent in all templates, defined formally by the addition of the third person singular -s, as in Jill walks

verb phrase: a constituent consisting of a group of words functioning as a verb

verbal: a form, such as a gerund, participle, or infinitive, made from a verb but functioning as a noun or modifier

voice: a quality of a transitive verb template indicating whether the subject acts (active voice) or is acted upon (passive voice)

Index